Teaching TV Quiz Shows
Wendy Helsby

Contents

Organisation of the Topic

Have I Got News For You

Teaching TV Quiz Shows begins with a short history and is then divided into the key media concepts of audiences, producers, textual analysis and genre. Debates around quiz shows such as representation and popular culture follow. Finally the focus moves to activities in preparation for the controlled test. There is also a brief scheme of work and Glossary.

Although the sections are treated as relatively discrete, inevitably there are interconnections between sections and where there are useful links to be made these are indicated. Each section has short activities to reinforce points and the key concepts. It is possible to cover the concepts simultaneously with a case study approach; for example, to use *The Weakest Link* as a starting point; or to take the concepts in a different order – such as doing genre first.

Although some quiz shows are very long running some may not currently be being broadcast whilst new ones are tried out. For example at the time of writing (2008) *Duel* had just started on ITV. For this reason the case studies used here have tended to focus on the longer running series or those which are important in relation to issues and debates.

Resources

For the teacher the first resource is to record a range of quiz shows off-air. Here student knowledge of quizzes as well as listings will be useful. In fact a pile of weekly listings magazines is an excellent resource to have for primary research such as on institutions, scheduling and audiences.

If you can, make a trip to become part of the audience of a quiz show. Television companies are often looking for audiences as well as participants. However be aware most shows require audiences to be over 16 or 18 years depending on the show.

There are websites to find out about being an audience for shows such as:

www.bbc.co.uk

www.beonscreen.com/uk/user/all-game-show-quiz-shows.asp

Apart from television shows currently available, two films which might be useful for this topic are *Quiz Show* (1994, Robert Redford) and *Starter For Ten* (2006, Tom Vaughan).

Web sites and other references are listed where relevant.

Introduction

'Your Starter for Ten'

Like soaps and sitcoms, quiz shows have been popular with television almost since it began. They have been called 'the great indigenous television forms' (Goodson quoted in Creeber, 2002, p.79), part of the staple diet of television proving popular with both audiences and producers. They are on most of the major terrestrial television channels and have recently morphed into phone-ins, on-line competitions, and other forms as **convergence** of media occurs. There are several reasons for this popularity: they are cheap to make once you have got the formula right; they are easy and quick to produce with a small crew as the personnel know the format and just repeat everything in a sort of an assembly line production; there is no change of set/location/presenter, only the contestants; several shows can be recorded in batches with the same studio audience; they are interactive for the home audience and provide various forms of pleasure.

Two Approaches

The theories used to look at the media can be divided into two broad camps. Firstly, there is a **political-economic** view which states that power is in the hands of the producers and ultimately the owners of the media. This would suggest that the media manipulates its audiences for profit whilst supporting the status quo and dominant ideologies held by those people in power. They would accommodate subordinate groups – a process of **hegemony** (see Glossary). This is in contrast to the second view, a **socio-liberal** approach which suggests that the media is representative of society and that there are many (pluralist) views possible, especially with the new digital technology. The audiences actively use the media for their own purposes and so can challenge this hegemony; this is a bottom up approach. These two approaches underpin the study of the media

Popular Entertainment – Perspectives

Mass entertainment has always been a site for ambivalent attitudes. The tabloid press and politicians frequently use popular cultural forms such as soaps and quizzes as a reason to criticise the media (and Media Studies). But this popularity tells us much about the mediated social world in which we (and the press and politicians) exist. Why are quiz shows criticised? There are many reasons. Some see them as trivial, promoting materialistic attitudes and playing on greed. Others see them as anti-intellectual based on information that is mechanistic (like knowing the dates of the kings and queens of England) rather than understanding concepts. A socio-economic view would say that they underline the education system of testing as a measure of success and therefore support the dominant beliefs about what is an educated person. In addition they perpetuate the belief (**ideology**) that we can all achieve, that we all have equal opportunity to win; thus, helping to maintain social differences. In discussing quiz shows Fiske (1987, p.266) suggests that 'Cultural capital, like economic capital, is presented as being equally available to all, but is actually confined to those with class power.'

Others (social-liberal) would see the way that audiences use the quiz shows for different purposes, such as entertainment or learning new facts, as participatory, gratifying different needs. The audience would be active in decoding and reading the text.

See Activity 1a: Two Points of View

NOTES:

1.1 Definition

Before you start to study this topic it is important that the definition of 'Television Quiz Show' is clear. Television quiz shows can be seen as a **sub-genre** of game shows having similar qualities such as winners and losers, prizes and audience participation. Other conventions associated with both quiz and game shows are: a personality who hosts the show, glamorous assistants, live audiences, competition, tension and catch phrases. These are quite broad conventions so we need to differentiate between the various types of show. What makes a programme a quiz rather than a game show? There is much slippage between quiz and game and where each begins and ends is often blurred. Mittell (2004, p.35) talks about a narrow view of the sub-genre as: 'High-minded contestants answer intellectual questions in an allegedly "honest" competition for a large prize of cash and merchandize'. As we shall see the boundaries of this definition have been considerably stretched. In fact we could start by questioning 'high-minded', 'intellectual' and 'honest' for some of the quiz shows that have been on television.

The definition used here is that quiz shows rely only upon knowledge revealed through question and answer; whereas game shows can incorporate all types of activities in which knowledge and information are not key factors. The work of some media theorists can help us to begin to define the difference between quiz and game. Fiske (1987) discusses **Levi-Strauss'** work which distinguishes between games and rituals. This is not an easy distinction and if you want to explore this definition further you will need to see Fiske's full discussion. Levi-Strauss stated that in games everyone starts as equal but at the end there are winners and losers. However, in rituals different groups are made equals. For Fiske quiz shows are primarily games but with rituals at the beginning and end. In this definition the idea of showing knowledge is mixed with the tension of a game which may not require knowledge. In quizzes the knowledge of the contestant is pitted not just against the anonymous education system as in an exam, but against another individual(s). This gladiatorial setting adds excitement. The presenter combines the role of providing fun and excitement with the role of the schoolteacher – they have the right answer, and are in control of the ritual processes. They perform this ritual function particularly at the beginning and at the end of the quiz. In **Propp**'s terms (see Glossary) we could say the presenter has the ritual role of sender on a quest for answers.

1.2 Audience Appeal

Most people like quizzes, games and puzzles: some of us like word games such as crosswords and Scrabble; whilst others like number games such as Sudoku. As a child you have probably played Trivial Pursuit and other games where you have to use your intelligence and knowledge to play. You might have done quizzes in magazines and maybe even entered competitions.

See Activity 1b: Your Quiz Likes and Dislikes

It is probably true that the most attractive element is the **interactive** nature of quizzes. A report in 2000 claimed that one in ten Britons describe themselves as quizaholics and four out of five compete with contestants when watching TV quizzes (Hill, 2000). Pub quizzes and charity quiz nights attest to the popularity of participating in quizzes as do specialised internet sites.

Television quiz shows are globally popular. They range from big spectacle shows where contestants can win huge sums of money to low key shows like *Venntieventi* (*Twenty-Twenty*) in Italy: '"Very tame stuff. They win pretty inconsequential amounts of money. There is neither the tension nor the spectacle of the big television quiz shows. We are trying to do something intelligent and sophisticated. A programme in whispers and measured tones....This is not trash television not even trendy television. This is a programme with minimal costs and low key setting"' (Mirabella, host of the show, in Coppini, *The Guardian, Europe*).

The quiz show genre is seen as a 'legitimate and culturally valued form of broadcasting' (Mittell, 2004, p.31) in many cultures.

1.3 Conclusion

Although quizzes, conundrums, puzzles and games were around before the advent of the mass media, the formula of the broadcast quiz show does not appear to have its roots in earlier mass media. The quiz show, like soaps and sitcoms, is one of the few indigenous broadcasting genres. In the middle of the twentieth century it had to be designed for the new medium of the wireless and then television. Now it is a mainstay of broadcasting. In studying it we will begin by looking more closely at its history.

So, fingers on buzzers please!

Introduction

References

Coppini, G. 'Dead Exciting Game Shows', *The Guardian, Europe*.

Creeber, G. (ed.) (2002) *The Television Genre Book*, London: bfi.

Fiske, J. (1987) *Understanding Television*, London: Methuen.

Gramsci, A. (1971) *Selections from the Prison Notebooks*. London: Lawrence and Wishart.

Hill, A. 'Focus: Q: Why Do We Love Quizzes? A: Because They Fulfil a Need for Knowledge in Society and They're Fun', *The Observer*, 5 November 2000. InfoTrac; Thomson Gale.

Mediafile (1991) Mary Glasgow Publications Ltd., Series 4, Issue 1.

Mittell, J. (2004) *Genre and Television. From Cop Shows to Cartoons in American Culture*, London: Routledge.

NOTES:

Activity 1a: Two Points of View

Read the following quotation:

> '…fostering a morally unhealthy attitude toward money, rewarding trivial displays of knowledge and engaging participants in exploitative and "degrading" performances' (Holmes, 2005).

- Apart from quiz shows, what other types (**genre**) of television programme could this comment refer to?
- Name some television shows that you think may be criticised in such a way.

You might have included a range of programmes from reality shows such as *Big Brother* through game shows like *Deal or No Deal*. These programmes have strong similarities to quiz shows in that they reward competitiveness even if it is indirect, and have a 'winner'. They are seen as exploiting performances of both ordinary people and celebrities.

- Now take the opposite view: What would be your *defence* of these programmes?

Activity 1b: Your Quiz Likes and Dislikes

- List as many games and activities you have played. Is your list long or short? Try to analyse what you like(d) about these games. What pleasures did you get from playing games or doing quizzes? Is it because you are competitive and like winning? Is it because you enjoy the interaction with others or challenging yourself?
- What do you not like about these activities? Is it because you feel they are pointless? Do you feel that the odds are stacked against you winning?.
- Is there anyone you know who enjoys quizzes? They may belong to a pub quiz team for example or regularly do charity quizzes? If so, do some (primary qualitative) research. Interview them and ask them why they enjoy this activity.

Keep your answers to this research and also from 1a as you will find it useful when you study audiences in more detail.

History of Quiz Shows

Have a Go!

The precursors of TV quiz shows can be traced back to radio or the 'wireless'.. In Britain, the BBC claimed that the 1937 *Inter-regional Spelling Competition* in Children's Hour represented the birth of the 'quiz programme' on British radio, although Holmes (2005) suggests that when this claim was made it was probably more an attempt by the BBC to capture the moral (and educational) high-ground from ITV.

By the 1940s quiz interludes on radio were part of general entertainment shows such as Wilfred Pickles *Have a Go!*, where there were small cash prizes – 'Give 'em the money Mabel' was a catch phrase (Mabel was Pickles' on stage helper and real life wife). Or they were of a more serious intellectual intent such as *Animal, Vegetable or Mineral* in which the participants were well known intellectuals and academics who pondered questions posed to them by a question master on articles from the British Museum, whilst the listeners followed their powers of deduction and were overawed by their knowledge. However, quiz shows as we recognise them today and as popular entertainment really started in the USA.

It is important to understand the basic differences between British and American broadcasting. This is discussed more fully below, but briefly: British broadcasting on radio began in the 1920s and was financed by a licence fee paid on each radio set, and controlled as a public service to inform, educate and entertain, by a government appointed body, the BBC Board of Governors (now the BBC Trust, 2007). BBC television followed this structure. Commercial television (ITV) began in 1955 and was funded by advertising but still with a public service ethos. Official commercial radio started even later in the 1970s. Today British media are undergoing change as a result of de-regulation, convergence and fragmentation.

In America broadcasting has in the main always been funded by advertising and sponsorship, and owned and controlled by commercial organisations. Its ethos therefore is to make a profit through entertaining the public and to deliver the biggest audience as possible to advertisers and sponsors.

2.1 Quiz Shows in America

The popularity of the quiz show in America was quite a phenomenon. They began on local radio as early as 1923 with *The Pop Question Game* (Mittell, 2004) and were regularly part of other shows during the Depression of the 1930s giving listeners a chance to win prizes. The informality of the (apparently) unscripted responses and the promise of monetary prizes meant that by 1940 there were 50 quiz shows on radio in the USA and by the end of the 1940s there were 200 (figures from www.pbs.org/wgbh/amex/quizshow). Because these shows were all on commercial radio they were funded by sponsors or individual producers. This meant that pressure could be put on contestants and presenters to toe the commercial line. For example, on *Information, Please*, which required the audience to send in questions to try to stump a panel of experts, the sponsors Reynolds Tobacco Company demanded that panellists smoked its cigarettes. In fact many of the shows were heavily scripted and like their later television counterparts ran into criticisms for this.

After the war the quiz show's popularity grew and as television began to emerge as the preferred option for domestic entertainment the quiz show moved across. Some radio quiz shows made the direct transition from sound to audio-visual. However, once you could see the programme rather than just hear it, there were new requirements which the shows needed to fulfil, such as how the contestants looked on the screen. Most television quiz shows were scheduled in off peak time as they tended to be cheap productions used as fillers in the schedules, except for shows like *The $64,000 Question* which had a huge potential prize. The big prize quiz shows hit prime time and were some of the

NOTES:

most popular shows on television in the 1950s until tainted by fraud. However, in spite of such setbacks the quiz show format has proved to be one of the most resilient on television.

Twenty-One, featured in the film *Quiz Show*...

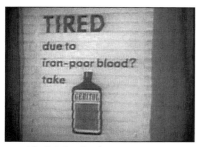

...and Geritol, the show's sponsor

$64,000

The $64,000 Question (CBS 1955–8) produced by Joseph Cates was the first big prize television show. The prize was equivalent to about half a million dollars today. Like many of the early television quiz shows this had started on radio when it was called *Take it or Leave it*. So ubiquitous was the television title *The $64 Question* that it entered into the lingua franca and people would say 'that's the $64,000 question' about any problem that arose for which the answer was not obvious or easy.

When it had originally begun on radio the top prize was $64 and it ran for ten years with no hike in this prize. Once on television the stakes were raised. This rise in prize money inevitably increased the tension for the contestants who could now be viewed under the spotlight as they made a decision which could make them wealthy or leave them with nothing. On one show 55million people tuned in (that's just under the total population of Great Britain) and 15,000 people wrote in weekly to apply to be on the show.

See Activity 2a: The medium

By the end of the 1950s the popularity of *The $64,000 Question* led to a huge increase in the number of television quiz shows on American television. The stakes were so high in these shows that it led to the potential for fraud and there were several high profile cases where the producers were seen to be helping certain contestants. So extraordinary was the rise and fall

of this type of quiz show that a film was made by Robert Redford (*Quiz Show*, 1994) about an infamous scandal in the *Twenty-One* quiz show of the 1950s.

See Activity 2b: The Quiz Show

2.2 Early Television Quiz Shows in Britain: The BBC

As mentioned above Britain had a different broadcasting structure to that of the USA. Radio as a national broadcast medium began when the BBC was established in 1927 as a Public Service Broadcaster. Television had started broadcasting, although to only a small area, in 1936 but had to cease in 1939 with World War 2 and didn't restart until 1946. Its structure followed that of BBC radio. That is, it was a public service broadcaster which was paid for by a licence fee. (PSB is further discussed in Section 4). The Board of Governors was responsible for its regulation. Its ethos was built largely on the Reithian ideals of informing and educating the public as well as entertainment (John Reith had been the first Director General of the BBC when it was established in 1927 and had very strong moral ideas about what broadcasting should be about). In order to retain its independence from commercial pressures there was no advertising on any programme, not even unpaid advertising. It would certainly have considered using large sums of public money for prizes as something not to be encouraged and which could be seen as being profligate with the public's licence money.

As in America, quiz programmes early on were built upon successful ones from radio. The first quiz show on British television was probably *Spelling Bee* hosted by Freddie Grisewood who also had the same role on radio when the show was first broadcast in 1938. Similar shows had an educational tone with well known academics answering questions, such as in *The Brains Trust* which had started on radio in 1941. Some shows used the general public: *What Do You Know* (1946) was a quiz show which again began on radio where the contestants competed for the title of 'Brain of Britain'. This became the quiz's title in 1967 and it is still going as *Brain of Britain* on Radio 4. Contestants play in regional qualifiers with the winner becoming Brain of Britain. A variation on this is *Round Britain Quiz* (1947–) a regional team quiz, which also survives on radio. A general knowledge quiz for school children was called *Top of the Form* (1947) in which each school provided four pupils of different ages as a team.

Some of these formats made a direct transition from radio to television such as *Top of the Form* (BBC 1953–75). *Brain of Britain* moved to

History of Quiz Shows

television in 1967 where it was called *Ask me Another* and *The Brains Trust* (BBC 1951–61) also moved across. But none of these survive today on television. Television's *Mastermind* (BBC 1972–) and *University Challenge* (1962–) are in a similar style of intellectual general knowledge quiz shows.

What Do You Know?

A variation was to have celebrity panellists and these were introduced early on. *What's My Line* (BBC 1952–62, 1973 –4; Thames 1984–90) was a popular show which was called a quiz show but was more in the line of a parlour game. It consisted of celebrities like the irascible Gilbert Harding trying to guess the occupation of people from a mimed action. Other contemporary examples of celebrity quizzes are *A Question of Sport* (BBC 1970–), *Never Mind the Buzzcocks* (1996–) and *QI* (2002–).

An important milestone in the quiz genre in British television was the first show to offer money as a prize. In fact it was a BBC programme *The Charlie Chester Show* (BBC 1951–60) which was a light entertainment show hosted by the comedian Charlie Chester. It had a game sequence called Pot Luck in which participants played for prizes (and forfeits). Remember these earlier shows all began on BBC because there was no other broadcaster in the United Kingdom until 1955.

See Activity 2c: Is the Medium the Message?

2.3 British Television: Commercial Television

Quiz shows with general public participants were really to flourish with commercial television (ITV) which started in the UK in 1955. The advent of television funded by advertisements and with shareholders wanting profits signalled a whole new approach to entertainment. Although based upon the US system, commercial television in the UK was much more highly regulated. Like the BBC it had to follow a PSB (public service broadcasting) remit to educate, entertain and inform its audience. However, it was the forms of entertainment which were much broader in their appeal that differentiated the programme content

of commercial television from the BBC. The worthiness of the BBC was deemed too elitist and the owners of commercial television such as the Grade brothers with ITV wanted to appeal to a much wider demographic base. To this end they introduced formats that had already proved successful in the States like the quiz show which offered the opportunity for big money prizes rather than just the kudos of winning which generally had been the format of BBC quiz shows: commercial television 'ushered in a major shift in the manifestation of popular taste' (Whannel, 1992: 182) and a shift in the popularisation of television culture in general (see Sendall, 1982 and Holmes, 2005).

Take Your Pick and *Double Your Money* were ITV's first quiz shows and appeared in the first year; by 1957 there were eight per week (Whannel, 1992). *Double Your Money* hosted by Hughie Green with his trans-Atlantic twang evoked this new commercialism. Audience participation shows proved a winning formula in the UK as they had done in America. The importance of knowledge though became less important than the entertainment factor of the 'game' so the conflation of quiz and game shows occurred.

The debate even then was that such programmes 'dumbed down' television and exploited audiences' voyeuristic tendencies. As Sue Holmes states 'the genre was attacked by critics for fostering a morally unhealthy attitude toward money, rewarding trivial displays of knowledge and engaging participants in "exploitative and degrading" performances' (2005). There was certainly debate in the contemporary press about the rights and wrongs of offering prizes, cash or in kind, to contestants. Concerns with the exploitative nature of the genre as it became more game show than quiz show were raised: 'watching one man in a large arena being baited. The Roman gladiator faced a lion…And, in the age of television, chosen members of a live audience confront the Quiz master' (Anant, 1955: 27, quoted in Holmes, 2005). The gladiatorial aspect of winners and losers, and how the latter could be humiliated and the former lauded, is of course still present today.

See Activity 2d: Research

The popularity of the quiz show with both producers and audiences has meant that they have survived many changes both in form and style, but their basic appeal remains the same. Why do audiences enjoy quiz shows? Section 3 picks up on this point.

References

Holmes, S. (2005) *The Quiz/Show in British TV History*, 23 December, www.birth-of-tv.org/birth/.

Holmes, S. (2006) in *Media, Culture and Society*, Vol. 29 (1): 53–74, London, Thousand Oaks and New Delhi: Sage Publications.

www.pbs.org 'The American Experience/Quiz Show Scandal/People &Events/The Rise of TV Quiz Shows'. www.pbs.org/wgbh/amex/quizshow (accessed 12 October 2008).

NOTES:

Student Activities

Activity 2a: The Medium

The producer of *The $64,000 Question* Cates said, 'It couldn't have happened in any other medium' (in Holmes, 2005).

What do you think he meant by this comment? Consider the special characteristics of television which made him say this.

Activity 2b: The Quiz Show

You could view the film *Quiz Show* at this point. (This film can also be used for studying areas such as regulation and debates about representation.)

What similarities and differences do you see in the format of quiz shows from the 1950s to today? Make a table with elements such as presenter, set, contestants, etc. to help you do the comparison.

Extension Activity

Discuss how far you believe commercial pressures influence programme-makers.

Activity 2c: Is the Medium the Message?

What difference does it make to see rather than just hear?

- Try listening to part of a quiz show that you have never seen without any pictures.

What does your mind do whilst listening?

Make a mental image of the studio set.

What impressions do you have of the contestant from their voices and the words they use?

What do you feel about the presenter? Does their style infer a particular type of person; for example, the presenter has a northern accent and sounds friendly and jovial but not very intelligent?

Give reasons for your opinions.

- Now watch the extract.

Does watching it change your opinion of any of the points made? If so how?

Discuss clothing, mannerisms, accents, gender, age, and so on, and how they may influence attitudes.

How does seeing influence tension and drama which are elements that all quiz shows rely upon?

Return to this exercise once you have studied representation and discuss further the issues about representation this type of research uncovers.

Student Activities

Activity 2d: Research

Do some research on past quiz shows. Ask parents and grandparents if they can remember any show they enjoyed.

Here are some of the quiz games that have been (and some still are) popular which might help jog their memories:

- *Raise The Roof* (ITV) – Contestants used general knowledge to become the final two who were then put in sound proof booths. A house worth £100,000 was the prize.

- *Wheel of Fortune* (ITV) – Contestants answered general knowledge questions. If right they spun the wheel and won a prize. Prizes up to £20,000 could be won.

- *Big Break* (BBC) – Three professional snooker players teamed up with three members of the public who answered questions to win time for the players to pot balls. Exotic holidays or cash prizes were on offer. There was another similar show but with darts players.

- *Countdown* (C4) – Contestants make words and sums from letters and numbers. Series champion could win the Oxford English Dictionary (£3,000).

- *Bruce's Price is Right* (ITV) – Six contestants answered questions on the price of a wide range of goods. Exotic holiday and commodities could be won.

- *Telly Addicts* (BBC1) – Two teams played rounds of questions about TV shows. Prizes included holidays and audio-visual equipment.

- *Family Fortunes* (ITV) – Two families had to guess top answers from different surveys. Prizes included £3,000 and car.

(Teacher's note: If the activities suggested in Section 1 were completed the information gathered could be used in combination with work done in this section.)

Introduction

Why do people watch and participate in these shows even if only as part of the domestic audience? Can you really die of excitement on a quiz show? Stefano Aluigo a retired steelworker from Genoa was struck down by the excitement of getting through on the telephone to take part in his favourite television quiz show *Ventieventi* (*Twenty-Twenty*). Aluigi had been trying to get on the programme for weeks and had spent two hours on the night that he was successful. He had three questions to answer but the tension got to him and he unfortunately died. (Coppini, *The Guardian Europe*).

See Activity 3a: Q and A

There are some significant elements about audiences which your research will probably confirm. One important element for the audience of the quiz show is **interactivity**: '…the capacity of the home audience to participate in one fashion or another, in the game. That's vital….You've got to involve the audience to the degree that they're testing themselves on the game to see if they can play it. …they're involved because they're identifying with one of the contestants, or because they're emotionally involved, like spectators at a sporting event' (American producers quoted by Goedkoop, in Rose, 1984, p.297).

This means that the audience participate **vicariously** (second-hand) whilst watching from their armchair in the winning and losing of the contestants. What other pleasures could there be for audiences? Perhaps there is the pleasure of knowing the right answer and a sense of identification with the contestant. Maybe there is a **voyeuristic** pleasure of seeing a contestant under pressure and their reactions. Maybe there is the pleasure in watching someone winning. The quiz show encourages involvement, made even more possible today by digital 'red buttons'. *Test the Nation* (BBC 1), for example, allows teams of contestants to participate in the studio but also home viewers to send in answers by selecting options. This interactivity increases our interaction with the quiz as home audiences and identification with contestants, as well as our rivalry with them – isn't beating the contestant to the answer a source of pleasure? Another way to research audience interaction with quiz shows will be discussed later in the section.

See Activity 3b: Primary Qualitative Research

3.1 TV Quiz Audiences

Quiz shows have grown to be part of the staple diet of television. In a BFI survey on the top 100 lifestyle/light entertainment programmes on television second place was *Who Wants to be a Millionaire*. But another surprising aspect of this top 20 was the appearance of three quiz series in the top 5. 'We also appear to like our quiz shows not only to be entertainment but also to be serious and cerebral. How else can you explain *University Challenge* and *Mastermind* at numbers 4 and 5, both of them old war horses dating from the 1960s and 1970s' (www.bfi.org.uk/featurestv/100/articles/lifestlye).

To try to find out what audiences feel about quiz shows it is quite useful to look at comments made on web sites. But do remember these are self-selecting contributors. They cannot be used to make generalised comments but only to illustrate certain points about audiences. Here are some comments from people on the BBC web site after the first million was won on a quiz show:

'My main objection is that really difficult quizzes… only gain the winner …some ornament…[whilst] facile competitions … are rewarded with large amounts of cash.'

'Perhaps it is a reflection on the mediocre social life and physical surroundings in which most Brits find themselves.'

'Quiz programmes are a waste of licence payers' money.'

'As a teenager I think that these shows help in enhancing one's general knowledge.'

'Such programmes emphasise the way in which success in life can be a matter of chance rather than hard work.'

'I think quiz shows are great, they give people the opportunity to win things that you could only ever dream of.'

'Undoubtedly TV is being dumbed down. There is nothing wrong with wallpaper TV as long as this is balanced by programmes that make people think.'

'…difference between quality quiz programmes and game shows…people compete purely for the prestige of winning…in the second it is a chance to win large amounts of money.'

'Promote materialism and the growing gap between rich and poor.'

(www.news.bbc.co.uk)

See Activity 3c: Audience Comments

Section 3

What evidence is there about how audiences interact with quiz shows? Media researchers and psychologists have hypothesised about this. John Fiske said that they attract audiences through the 'ritual' of the programme which brings together shared meanings. The ritual ceremonies are presented in the introductions, the choreography, the *mise-en-scène* like the desks and the catch phrases, such as 'You are the weakest link'. There is a sense of the suspension of normal life, where 'the constraints of the everyday are evaded and its power relations are temporarily reversed' (Fiske, 1987) so ordinary people can become heroes.

In addition audiences are particularly active in quiz shows. They are 'live' events although of course pre-recorded in bunches. This appearance of immediacy allows the game to feel more exciting. Like a football match we find it more enthralling to see the actual game rather than a recording. After all if it is a recording the result is already known. What's the fun of taking part even as an audience if the game is over? The sense of the present is therefore important.

Another point is one made by a psychologist who stated that 'People now feel entitled to their 15 minutes of fame and that combined with the current get-rich-quick attitude, means the ideas of appearing on television to compete for these huge cash prizes is appealing to our society like never before' (Wilson, quoted in Hill, 2000, p.20).

There are several points here which indicate why quiz shows are popular:

- The chance to be famous – to be on television.

- The excitement of the score – who is winning/losing.

- The immediacy – the sense of now.

- The chance to become successful and not ordinary.

- The knowledge of how the genre works, the pattern, the formula.

- The entertainment/education binary

opposition in the genre.

- 'The unrehearsed, unwritten ending' (Mittell, 2004, p.43) – not automatically knowing who will succeed.

- Unpredictability about whether a question will be answered links in to the vicarious pleasure of being able to answer at home or not – but of never losing.

3.2 General Audience Theories

There are more general theories which can be applied following two basic approaches to audiences. One suggests that audiences are **passive** receivers of knowledge and ideas. This means that they will reflect what they consume in their beliefs and actions. This 'hypodermic model' is now held to be too simplistic by most media researchers. However, it is the one that politicians and the tabloid press often use to scapegoat certain areas of the media. Classic recent examples have been rap music lyrics, computer games, girls' magazines all of which it has been claimed have influenced behaviour. This media **effects** model has been refined to a two-step model where information and ideas are given through a particular party such as a teacher or journalist or media presenter and this modifies the message and allows it to be delivered more subtly. It uses such ideas as de-sensitisation and cultivation.

The second main approach is that audiences are **active** and can read and use texts to gratify needs (**uses and gratification** theories). The audience can understand the same text differently as they decode so we can talk about 'audiences' in the plural. The reading of the text will depend upon many variables such as age, gender, class, interests, race, ethnicity and experience. This is a **pluralistic** approach to the media. With the active audience theory the audience does have the power to reject representations or messages. It is seen as a two-way process between audience and producer.

NOTES:

However, mass media texts do target mass audiences and do encourage a '**preferred reading**', even though there are different readings possible such as negotiated and oppositional readings (Stuart Hall and also David Morley's seminal work on the *Nationwide* audience, 1980). The targeted audience is constructed by codes and conventions and encouraged to read the text in the way that the producer wishes. How is this done?

Firstly, there are the generic codes and conventions. These are recognised by audiences. Secondly, the repetition of ideas which are implicit in the way the shows are organised and the type of contestants and knowledges rewarded. These may provide or confirm underlying beliefs or 'myths' about society. We can see this perhaps most clearly in the issue of representation (see Section 7 on debates).

Thirdly, the quiz show will have a studio audience or contestants who reflect their target audience so the home audience is **inscribed** within the text (i.e. the show). Fourthly, unlike in a drama or documentary in viewing quiz shows the impression is that we are interacting with the medium. Television directs itself outward to the viewer: 'In those instances in which contestants are selected from the studio audience, they are plucked from among "us"… we constantly shift from one viewer position to another, collapsing the distance between contestants and ourselves as we answer along with them, falling back into the role of studio audience as we assess contestant prowess and luck (or lack thereof), assuming a position superior to both when we know more than they' (Allen, 1987).

In order to achieve the preferred readings the audience is positioned to be addressed by the text. The editing, the camera position, lighting, tone, pace and type of vocabulary used, all contribute to construct and position the audience or to inscribe them within the text.

In a quiz show this is particularly helped by the camera which is positioned to put us as a participant in the 'hot seat', or as an observer watching the contestant. We might be part of the studio audience or feel that we can view all from a 'deus ex machina', god-like, point of view. This space that we occupy is linked to ways of seeing. How are we asked to view the contestant and the presenter for example? Are they 'really stupid' or are we asked to admire them? These types of positioning have ideological significance as audience identities are constructed by the text.

3.3 What do Audiences do with Quiz Shows?

What psychological profiles can we see in audiences? We know audiences use the media for different purposes and different genres have different uses. The quiz show could have the following uses:

- Escapism – an escape into a fantasy world.

- Social cohesion – your friends watch the same show, or you can identify with the situation portrayed.

- Vicarious pleasures – exploring different emotions such as winning and losing.

- Reassurance – the formula never changes. You know what is going to happen.

- Emotional responses – there are different emotions, often humour, suspense and excitement.

- Identification – there is the belief that you could take part, that they are only ordinary people like yourself. You can identify with them and their backgrounds.

- Reaffirming beliefs – about ideas such as education and class.

Researchers have explored what audiences do with quiz shows: McQuail, Blumer and Brown (1972) in their study of television audiences and quiz programmes found that there were broadly similar uses. Most of the audiences used quiz programmes for four main gratifications:

1. Self-rating.

2. Social interaction.

3. Excitement.

4. Education.

McQuail also discovered that most of those who used quiz programmes for self-rating gratifications lived in council houses (owned by the Local Authority) and were working class. Why should this be so? Do you think they were using quiz programmes to provide themselves with an educational status which their own education may not have given them? This shows the media being used to compensate for some form of social lack. We can perhaps see this also with lonely people using soaps as a surrogate family/community. So the uses and gratification model of an active audience could be applied.

Others used it as part of their social networking so that they could talk to friends and acquaintances about the programme. They were supplementing other sources of need gratification. The excitement appeal was reported most often by working class viewers who were not very sociable so again compensating for lack

Section 3

of excitement in their lives. The educational appeal as a major gratification was most marked in people who had left education at the minimum age.

What do these findings tell you about the main audiences for quiz shows when this research was carried out?

See Activity 3d: Uses and Gratification – McQuail's groupings

3.4 Interactivity and Identity

Other research has been done on audiences and has discovered different profiles. A BBC Viewer Research report showed that audiences listening to quizzes such as *What Do You Know?* not only played along with the quiz attempting to answer the questions but also admired the capabilities of the participants: '"all utter marvels"; "a really remarkable performance"; "a truly brilliant brain"' (12 July 1962, quoted in Holmes, 2006, p.67). Whilst a more recent report stated that, 'Research suggests that four out of five people compete with the contestants when watching TV quizzes,' (Thomson Gale, 2000) and that 'Men are six times more likely to describe their general knowledge as well above average' (ibid.). Does this indicate the type of audience or contestant that might take part in a quiz show?

Quiz shows were once called 'audience participation' shows and this indicates how interactivity was and still is significant. The *Brains Trust*, for example, apparently had 3000 questions sent in from listeners every week (Holmes, 2006). Today quiz shows provide even more direct evidence of active audience participation particularly now that we have the 'red button', phone-ins and on-line responses.

'[B]y identifying with the winner we can share the sensation of winning – but we can also share the sadness and the disappointment of the losers which, perhaps, makes it easier to bear our own disappointments. The prime qualifications for being on most quiz shows are to look and sound "ordinary" so that mass audiences can identify with the contestant' (McQueen, 1998: 72) This also indicates the vicarious nature of the quiz shows.

These factors are important for the public service remit as they encourage interaction, involvement and identification with 'ordinary' contestants, and therefore viewers, and so help to justify the public funding. They are also important for commercial broadcasters who are delivering audiences to advertisers.

3.5 Quiz Shows and Audience Targeting

Remember the definition of the genre of quiz shows is not a water tight one, it 'leaks' into other types of shows such as game shows which are also 'audience participation'.

Clark (1987) identifies four types of game and quiz shows:

1. Specialist.

2. Intellectual.

3. Celebrity.

4. Populist.

Each appeals to a different type of audience.

See Activity 3e: Targeting Audiences

In Britain we are generally put into a class for statistical purposes by income and education and the traditional grouping is A, B, C1/C2, D and E.

In group E are people who watch a lot of television such as the unemployed and OAPs but who have very little income. D are lower working class, manual labourers, C2 are clerical workers,

NOTES:

C1 are people such as lower managers, supervisors, B are educated people such as journalists and teachers and A are successful business people, doctors and so on. Using these categories and the four types of quiz shows what conclusions can you draw about audiences for particular types of quiz shows?

There are other factors. Audiences are targeted through the schedules. Day time audiences are different from prime time and late night audiences. Additionally each channel has an audience profile. What do you think would be the stereotypical BBC1 and Channel 4 audience? Would they be different? Do the channels have different audience profiles for different times of the day? You can study more about these issues of scheduling and audiences by reading Section 4 Industries and Institutions.

3.6 New Ways of Taking Part

One of the most successful recent quiz programmes has been phone-ins. Here the audience can take direct part in quizzes by phoning in answers. There have been major concerns with this style of quiz programme and the regulators (Ofcom and the BBC) have stepped in to address the situation (see the Industries and Institutions Section 4). Other newer platforms for quiz shows are cable and digital channels. All of these have had problems with regulators. One of the reasons for the fuss is that these quiz shows appeal to poorer people who would not normally get on to a television show. More than half the viewers for ITV Play belonged to social category 'E' meaning they were pensioners or casual workers; 40% were over 65 and 70% were women. The audience of a show like *The Mint* (ITV Play) contained lots of young mothers, shift workers, students and older people ('Minted; TV quizzes. Ethics of ITV Quiz Shows', *The Economist* (US), 7 October 2007, p.38).

To summarise: audiences are active and participatory. They can be targeted and encouraged by various techniques. There are different reasons for audiences to like quiz shows.

This section should have provided you with the way you can investigate how audiences interact with the medium of television and the genre of quiz shows. Your own research will be invaluable in supplementing the points made here and illustrating audience differences. Perhaps the one key word to remember is 'interactivity'.

References

Allen, R. (1987) in Fiske, J. *Television Culture*, London: Routledge.

Clarke, M. (1987) *Teaching Popular Television*, London: Heinemann.

Coppini, G. 'Dead Exciting Game Shows', *The Guardian Europe*.

'Minted; TV Quizzes. Ethics of ITV Quiz Shows', *The Economist* (US), 7 October 2006, InfoTrack OneFile, Thomson Gale.

Fiske, J. (1987) *Television Culture*, London: Routledge.

Goedkoop, R. (1984) 'The Game Show', in Rose, B.C. (ed.) *TV Genres: A Handbook and Reference Guide*, London: Greenwood.

Hill, A. (2000) 'Q: Why do we love quizzes? A: Because they fulfil a need for knowledge in society and they're fun.' *The Observer*, 5 November 2000.

McQueen, D. (1998) *Television: A Media Student's Guide*, London: Arnold.

Morley, D. (1980) *The Nationwide Audience: Structure and Decoding*, London: British Film Institute.

Welsh, J. (2001) 'Textual Analysis for Beginners', *Media Studies Conference Papers*, London: British Film Institute.

Student Activities

Activity 3a: Q and A

Quiz shows require Questions and Answers.

The types of questions asked on quiz shows will depend upon the type of quiz show and this in turn may indicate the target audience.

Consider two or three shows with which you are familiar. Are the questions difficult or easy? Do they require specialist or general knowledge?

Are the questions and the knowledge they contain the real point of the shows? Is that why people watch them?

What other reasons could there be for watching someone else show off what they know? Brain storm ideas and put them down in a mind-map in the space below to refer back to as you study what others have said about audiences.

Activity 3b: Primary Qualitative Research

If you answered the questions in Sections 1 and 2 you have already begun to think about yourself as an audience and the reasons for doing quizzes.

Here is your chance to do some more primary research:

Do your family members like/dislike quiz shows?

Draw up a questionnaire to find out.

If everyone in your group does the same questionnaire you will come up with some useful data on audiences.

What types of question could you ask?

N.B. You will need to be very clear on your definition of TV quiz shows so that when you ask questions the respondents are clear about the type of programme you are studying.

Some questions you could ask to collect data are:

- Gender.
- Age.
- Channels watched.
- Quiz shows watched.
- How often watched.
- Why do you like them? For example, presenter, types of question, contestants, jokes, subject, etc.
- Are you an active viewer? Do you answer the questions with the contestants? Why?
- Do you dislike certain quiz shows? Why?

Compare your results with others.

Are there any points that reappear regularly?

You may perhaps find out if certain groups, e.g. parents or grandparents watch similar/different shows. These results will be important for talking about different target audiences and audience appeal.

Extension Activity

Now present your results as a chart for a report.

Student Activities

Activity 3c: Audience Comments

Consider the following comments, which were all posted on the BBC website by real-life quiz show viewers:

> 'My main objection is that really difficult quizzes… only gain the winner …some ornament…[whilst] facile competitions … are rewarded with large amounts of cash.'

> 'Perhaps it is a reflection on the mediocre social life and physical surroundings in which most Brits find themselves.'

> 'Quiz programmes are a waste of licence payers' money.'

> 'As a teenager I think that these shows help in enhancing one's general knowledge.'

> 'Such programmes emphasise the way in which success in life can be a matter of chance rather than hard work.'

> 'I think quiz shows are great, they give people the opportunity to win things that you could only ever dream of.'

> 'Undoubtedly TV is being dumbed down. There is nothing wrong with wallpaper TV as long as this is balanced by programmes that make people think.'

> '…difference between quality quiz programmes and game shows…people compete purely for the prestige of winning…in the second it is a chance to win large amounts of money.'

> 'Promote materialism and the growing gap between rich and poor.'

- Which comments from the BBC web site do you agree/disagree with? Tick for agree and cross for disagree. What does this reveal about your attitudes to quiz shows?

- Discuss the comments with others in your group.

Activity 3d: Uses and Gratification

Here is the list of questions asked in the survey of 'Gratification of Television Quiz Programmes', taken from McQuail *et al.*, 1972.

You might like to adapt this and ask a representative sample of people to help in your own research on audiences.

❑ <u>Cluster 1 Self-Rating Appeal</u>
I can compare myself with the experts.
I like to imagine that I'm on the programme doing really well.
I feel pleased that the side I favour has actually won.
I'm reminded of when I was in school.
I laugh at the contestant's mistakes.
Hard to follow.

❑ <u>Cluster 2 Basis for Social Interaction</u>
I look forward to talking about it with others.
I like competing with other people watching me.
I like working together with the family on the answers.
I hope the children will get a lot out of it.
The children get a lot out of it.
It brings the family together sharing the same interest.
It's a topic of conversation afterwards.
Not really for people like myself.

❑ <u>Cluster 3 Excitement Appeal</u>
I like the excitement of a close finish.
I like to forget my worries for a while.
I like trying to guess the winner.
Having got the answer right I feel really good.
I completely forget my worries.
I get involved in the competition.
Exciting.

❑ <u>Cluster 4 Educational Appeal</u>
I find I know more than I thought.
I feel I have improved myself.
I feel respect for the people on the television programme.
I think over some of the questions afterwards.
Educational.

❑ <u>Cluster 5</u>
It's nice to see the experts taken down a peg.
It is amusing to see the mistakes some of the contestants make.

❑ <u>Cluster 6</u>
I like to learn something as well as being entertained.
I like finding out new things.

❑ <u>Cluster 7</u>
I like trying to guess the answer.
I hope to find that I know some of the answers.

❑ <u>Cluster 8</u>
I find out the gaps in what I know.
I learn something new.
A waste of time.

Try these questions on different types of quiz audience, such as adults, children, teenagers, men, women and so on.
Compare your results with others. The bigger your sample the more accurate will be your conclusions.

Student Activities

Activity 3e: Targeting Audiences

Clark (1987) has identified four types of game show, listed below in the 'Category' column. In the middle column write a name of a quiz show that you feel represents this type of show. In the third column write the type of audience to which it might appeal and why. Try to indicate elements such as age, gender, race, ethnicity, interests, and class, as well as needs.

Category	Quiz Show	Audience
Specialist		
Intellectual		
Celebrity		
Populist		

The $64,000 Question

The industry is the business of the media and its different companies. It involves looking at who owns companies, how they are organised, the size of the companies and how this influences the outcomes in terms of television shows. The institutions are the working practices of its employees and the professional processes they go through to bring a programme to your screen. They will have certain values or ideas which are similar across a range of companies about what is good practice. In news, for example, we talk about 'news values' and being 'news worthy'. Journalists have a general sense of what is news worthy across a range of news outlets and so you tend to get similar stories on the same day across different media. They work using news values which again are a common currency within the profession.

As was stated in the Introduction quiz shows are part of the staple diet of television channels. This is partly because they are cheap for producers and partly because of their appeal to audiences. The people working in the industry have a sense of what they believe makes a good programme, what a presenter should do, what type of personality appeals and so on. Basically they understand what works within their channel and within the media in general. Channels build a brand identity. If you look at the 'idents' (their own trailers) of different channels you should be able to pick out the identity, the 'persona', that each channel wishes to give. They try to attract and retain the audience that this identity should appeal to partly through scheduling.

See Activity 4a: How Many? Quantify

4.1 Scheduling

Firstly, let us find out how the quiz show works in the television schedules.

As a genre the main costs are the sets, the presenters, the crew and the prizes. If there is a studio audience they are 'free'. A quiz show usually lasts about 30 minutes of broadcast time. Its broadcast time can vary from once a week to sometimes every evening. It is pretty obvious that sets and personnel are not going to be brought together for just 30 minutes once a week. This means that several shows will be recorded at one go in 'clusters'. The sets and personnel will be up and running so the programmes are more economical to record. Any show which is this cost effective is good news for the channel. We talk about production values for a programme. This reflects how much is spent on the major costs. High production values mean a lot of money is spent on the sets with more lights, music, bigger prizes. Low production values are reflected in cheap sets and less gloss. When you

are watching quiz shows how can you tell their production values?

In general quiz shows have low production values compared, for example, to dramas. But what about the big prize quiz shows? These have to justify their costs by attracting larger audiences and therefore if it is a commercial station more revenue from advertising or sponsorship.

The BBC as a PSB has to justify the use of its revenue from the public licence fee. It is for this reason that prizes on the BBC are generally not so high in monetary value as on commercial stations such as ITV.

See Activity 4b: Popularity

4.2 Fragmented Audiences

Television has to build a loyal audience in an increasingly crowded media environment with computer games, DVDs, the internet and other options. We may in the future not talk about broadcasters but **narrowcasters** or even **niche broadcasting**. The future of television is much debated amongst those at the cutting edge of technology. Convergence of delivery into one screen, the ability to view on the move through phones and the possibility of watching programmes out of time slots are all pushing our viewing habits away from the traditional schedules. Of course, time shifting, showing programmes through the internet, podcasting and home recording all make it possible to view at different times than the original transmission.

In the future television may only be a medium for areas such as news and special events. However, at the moment, television is still the main form of domestic entertainment and it has to follow a linear scheduling process. Quiz shows which have a large and wide appeal are important, like soaps, in the schedule 'game'.

Traditionally the day has been segmented so that programmes can be geared to different audiences. This makes it easier for advertisers on commercial television to find their target market and the producers on all channels to decide the mode of address of programmes.

4.3 Techniques

Schedulers need to attract the target audiences to the channel and try and maintain their loyalty as long as possible. In order to do this they use certain tactics.

They will air trailers for programmes. This has become quite sophisticated using cross channel voice-over announcements with graphics, visual

Institutions and Industries

clips and split screens.

They may try **pre-echo** which means putting on a less popular show before a popular one so that viewers who tune in early will see some of the less popular show and hopefully be tempted to stay with it.

Another technique is **inheritance** which means putting a new or less popular show after a popular one so that the audience is inherited onto the new show. Even with the remote controller we still tend to be a little lazy about switching channels.

Hammocking allows a scheduler to put on a new or less popular show between popular shows, so that viewers are not tempted to switch off or over.

These classic scheduling techniques are also used with **common junction points** where programmes start at the same time on different channels but the same broadcaster so that viewers can switch between them without missing part of the programmes.

Using these devices helps to build a loyal audience to a channel. In your research did you note any of these techniques being used around the scheduling of quiz shows?

See Activity 4c: Audience

See Activity 4d: Scheduling

4.4 Television as a Medium

In Section 2 we described how quiz shows began on broadcast radio and then moved into television easily and quickly and became a staple part of the television diet. In order to understand why this should be so this section looks in greater detail at the medium of television and how it works.

There are three basic ways in which television can be organised:

1. It can be a state controlled institution. This is how China and other similar governments work.

2. It can be commercial paid for by business through sponsorship and advertising. This is the format that the USA adopted.

3. It can be a Public Service not controlled by the vested interests of either the state or capital. This is the format originally adopted in Britain with the BBC.

How does public service broadcasting work?

In the 1920s the government decided that BBC radio should be regarded as a utility and a public service. It would be paid for by a licence fee on each wireless set – (there was no television). A Board of Governors (now The BBC Trust, 2007) appointed by the government was established to regulate it. A Director-General was put in charge. The first D-G was John Reith. As we noted in Section 2 on the history of quiz shows he had a particular view of this new world of broadcasting and how it could be used for the public good. He believed it should educate, inform as well as entertain. There was to be no advertising and big money prizes would have been seen as anti the Reithian PSB ethos.

When television began in 1936 (but stopped broadcasting from 1939–46 due to World War 2) this idea of PSB was transferred to the new medium. The BBC was the only channel broadcasting in the UK whereas in America there were already many different commercial channels both national and local. Quiz programmes on the BBC had to be seen as generally educational rather than for entertainment.

In 1955 the first ITV companies were established on a regional basis. These were commercial companies and as in America funded by advertising revenue. Their programming was heavily influenced by the American model. But

NOTES:

they still had to inform and educate and thus had a public service remit. For example, they did school programmes, serious dramas and documentaries as well as having extended news programmes. However, they also had to deliver audiences, large audiences, to advertisers. (There was no sponsorship at the time.) One way of doing this was to have more populist shows such as soap operas (*Coronation Street* started in 1960), and quiz and game shows.

The critics of commercial television had prophesised that commercial television would produce more light weight entertainment which threatened to 'dumb down' British broadcasting. Game and quiz shows seem to epitomise this with participants having to behave sometimes in ridiculous ways, and greed and gambling being exploited in some games such as *Double Your Money*. The Pilkington Report (1960s) was critical of the way that quiz shows were used in television to encourage greed and consumption. It may have been one of the contributory reasons why in 1964 the BBC got the third terrestrial television licence for BBC2.

Over the next decades other new terrestrial channels began, Channel 4 in 1982 and Channel 5 started broadcasting in 1997. These with BBC1 and ITV (Channel 3) were the five terrestrial channels. By the 1990s there were also cable and satellite companies (BSkyB), which were commercial channels relying on advertising revenue and subscription for funding.

In the 1980s the Conservative government's agenda was to privatise and to encourage free enterprise. The government wanted to de-regulate broadcasting and break up what they perceived as 'the cosy duopoly' between the BBC and ITV. They also saw the ITV as a hugely profitable business. The phrase often quoted was that it had a 'licence to print money'. As a result of the Peacock Report the 1990 Broadcasting Act was passed. The BBC was only marginally touched by this Act, although it was to have a new broom in the 1990s in the guise of John Birt, the Director General. He introduced 'producer's choice' which in effect meant reducing the BBC's budget on programming. The BBC also had to have at least 25% of its programming coming from independent production companies instead of all in-house. However, the BBC regulatory authority, the Board of Governors remained as did the licence fee to pay for programming. The cap on prizes which had been a stalwart of the public service ethos in quiz shows (contestants were supposed to go in for quizzes for the kudos not the money) was still part of the ethos.

However, the new regulatory body for commercial television, the ITC (Independent Television Commission) was given a much 'lighter' regulatory touch. In 1993 it abolished the money caps on prizes that the previous regulatory body (IBA) had imposed. 'The IBA had fixed as an absolute maximum a prize equal in value to the price of a small car – the star prize in the old quiz show *The Sale of the Century*. *Who wants to be a Millionaire?* is clearly operating in a very different environment' (Wayne, 2000, p.200).

The 1990 Broadcasting Act restructured the ITV companies who had to bid for their licences and therefore needed to be far more profitable to pay for these new licences. In the 90s the amount of money being paid out by the companies for their licences combined with a turn down in advertising revenue led to companies having to look for savings and for new sources of income as well as ways of attracting audiences. In addition the multiplying of channels meant that the advertising revenue was being spread even more thinly. As a result the government had to loosen the regulatory controls. For example programmes began to be sponsored such as *Inspector Morse* and *Coronation Street*. Sponsorship had always been around in American television but not in Britain because it was felt it would allow too much power over programming from the vested interests of the sponsors (see the example of the a cigarette firm in Section 2).

In addition to this re-structuring the Thatcherist beliefs that the market forces should dominate was said to lead to a mercenary 'grab all' attitude and led to quiz programmes such as *Millionaire* being popular with audiences because it reflected the social mores of the time. These factors amongst others led to higher prize money being offered to raise the stakes in the audience ratings war.

4.5 New Structures

Now of course with the digital opportunities there are many more channels available through cable and satellite companies, as well as the terrestrial broadcasters who also own digital channels.

ITV has been in financial difficulties particularly after the collapse of Ondigital, and the regional ITV companies eventually combined until a single company ITVplc finally appeared. Channel 4, which also has a public service remit, has been hoping to get some form of funding from the government and is looking avariciously at the BBC's licence money. It has lost a considerable income from the cancellation of phone-in quizzes. Channel 4 has planned to sell Ostrich Media the company which produces its Quiz Call programme (Rees, 22 October 2006).

Institutions and Industries

All of these economic and structural factors influence the types of programming we receive. But what does it all mean in relation to quiz shows? The channels all have to attract audiences whether to justify the licence fee or to provide revenue through delivering audiences to advertisers and/or sponsors. To this end popular and relatively cheap programming, such as reality shows, life-style programmes and soaps are a staple diet. The advantage of the quiz format is that it can be put out at any time of the day because it does not contain sex and violence, nor does it tend to encourage bad language and so it doesn't have to be broadcast after the 9 p.m. watershed when adult material is shown (there are some exceptions, usually featuring celebrities, such as *QI* and *Never Mind the Buzzcocks*). A quiz can go out in the middle of the day or in the early evening slot and not offend different types of audience such as young families or elderly people.

Quiz shows are also cheap to make and can be easily transferred into other markets – that is they can be sold to other countries. *The Weakest Link*, for example, went across to America and has been franchised over the world with Anne Robinson 'clones'. This means they are highly profitable if the formula travels. However, as prizes get bigger there are also implicit dangers in the way that competitions are run and the type of opportunities that are opened to cheat the system.

4.6 Regulation

These dangers were highlighted at the very beginning of broadcasting. In 1926 (the BBC started in 1927) a memo stated '…the conduct of competitions should be carefully considered by the Programme Board before they were entered into by any department, and that under any circumstances no more that one a month should be held' (Holmes, 2006, p.57).

Why do you think the Board was so concerned about such types of programme?

A producer in children's radio in the 1930s was still battling with the same type of prejudice or beliefs: 'competitions…in the nature of lotteries….are to be deprecated. I feel that the right kind of competition which stimulates thought and creates intelligent interest has something to recommend it' (ibid., quoted in Holmes, 2006, p.58).

See Activity 4e: Lottery

The effect of these concerns was to produce three basically different types of quiz shows. One was for the kudos of taking part and winning and this was represented by a certificate, a piece of glassware or other similar low value trophy. These shows tended to be on the PSB channels. The second was for prizes of a more pecuniary nature, money or gifts in kind such as holidays and cars. For the latter the emphasis was not on in depth knowledge but about entertainment and the tension of winning and losing something that might be life changing. These types of quiz shows tended to be on commercial television. Thirdly, there was the 'have a go' personality show where the reward was not the focus but the 'fun' in taking part. These appeared on all types of channel. It is the second type that has generally caused the most concern for regulators.

4.7 Phone-in Scandal

This scandal blew up into the public domain in 2007 following a BBC *Panorama* programme. They discovered that some quiz entrants had no chance of winning on such shows as *Breakfast TV*. Other irregularities began to emerge including in the BBC and there is currently (2007–8) an on-going investigation into phone-ins and their regulation. The regulator who is in charge of this is Ofcom which took over the role of the ITC. Premium rate telephones are regulated by another body, ISCTIS.

ITV introduced phone-in quiz shows where competitors phone in to give answers to relatively simple questions. Why should ITV and other commercial companies use this type of

NOTES:

programme? It is partly economic to replace lost revenue as a result of the proliferation of channels and lost advertising income. The companies get a percentage of the fee paid to the phone company by the caller. It is therefore in their interests to get as many phone calls as possible. Thousands of people paid premium rate phone calls with huge odds against them and sometimes with no chance of winning.

Often the questions are very simple to encourage as many people as possible to phone in. Many have regarded these competitions as unfair and exploitative, not to mention dumbed down. Following complaints made which were supported by *Panorama*'s investigation Ofcom looked at removing this type of phone-in competition from ITV1 and 2 by reclassifying them as adverts for phone lines. In addition the Gambling Commission examined them to see if in fact they were lotteries and as such a fifth of the profits should go to charity.

Channel 4 (which like the BBC is a public service channel but is funded by commercials) started Quiz Call a digital channel in 2005. Although a broadcaster/publisher with a PSB remit it was suffering in the new fragmented media world. The phone-ins provided a profitable source of income. In August 2007 Channel 4 scrapped all phone-in competitions. Channel 4 estimated that £2.2 million pounds were generated from calls that were not entered correctly in the *You Say We Pay* competition from September 2004 to February 2007. They offered a full refund and stated that any un-reclaimed refunds would be donated to Great Ormond Street Hospital Children's Charity. Channel 4's group finance director said that as a commercially funded public service broadcaster they had seen the premium rate competitions as legitimate programming given the popularity with viewers but that audience trust had been compromised.

4.8 Quizmania

This brief case study will explain how these phone-ins worked. *Quizmania*, a phone-in quiz show, asked people to put a word that might fit next to one on the television screen. If they chose one that was behind a board in the studio they won. The callers 'sound mostly drunk, or medicated, or lonely, or educationally subnormal' many of them mystifyingly offered the 'very same answer that has been tried and rejected ten times already.' Also, '*Quizmania* was a new form that didn't need to be watchable. It didn't have personalities, suspense or meaningful prize money. It did not need to attract many viewers to make a profit. It did not rely on commercials. As each call costs approximately 70 pence if you get around half a million every night you are not in the business of making television at all: you are

simply making money' (quotes from Aitkenhead, 1996, p.33).

Quizmania went out on ITV1 every night for three hours from December to March in 1995/6 and for three nights a week over the summer. *The Mint* took over from *Quizmania*. (On some days *The Mint* clocked up nearly as many hours of airtime on ITV as the news.)

ITV which broadcast shows like *The Mint* also had ITV Play and other phone-in quiz shows as well as those on ITV1 and 2, and they found these types of shows very profitable. ITV said that they monitored the number of calls and when someone had made 150 calls they stopped taking them having already warned that person about the number of calls they had made. However, the person already had to pay for that number of calls at premium rate, well over £100 (*The Economist*, 7 October 2006).

Of course, ITV was not the only channel to use this profitable niche genre and it wasn't only the commercial world that was to be accused of misleading audiences. All the major broadcasters had problems with the phone-ins. Even *Blue Peter* the flagship BBC children's programme had to admit to irregularities in some of its competitions. Examples of misleading the public with these types of competition included a fake contestant who was produced after a technical problem with the phone-in competition. In some cases viewers were phoning in when they had not been told that the lines were already closed. In other cases members of the production teams were given made-up names and announced on screen as winners.

See Activity 4f: Rigged Competitions

Shows such as *Brain Teaser* (Channel 5), ITV's *X-Factor*, Channel 4's *Richard and Judy* have been some of the shows tainted by accusations of phone-in irregularities. As a result the regulator Ofcom appointed auditors to look at these types of competition shows. This is quite a blow for the channels because phone-in quiz shows are very popular and profitable. Channel 4 said they got £9 million revenue and Channel 5 £6 million (Turner, *Hollywood Reporter*, 14 March 2007).

In March 2007 ITV announced that it was going to stop the ITV Play quiz channel. This followed the controversy with the phone-fee scandal of the terrestrial channels. This was a blow to ITV which had a considerable profit from these quiz shows; in 2006 it was £54 million.

The problems with these shows is that they are 'live' and are happening in real time so that any difficulties such as phone hitches can stall a programme. Another difficulty is that there are

Institutions and Industries

several organisations in the interactive chain getting the questions from the producers to the receivers and answers back to the producers any one of which could fail.

See Activity 4g: The Communication Line

See Activity 4h: Question

Rigging outcomes in quiz shows is not new. Producers have often controlled outcomes more effectively than most viewers suspect. Quiz shows need to be entertaining. *Stop the Music* for example had phone calls stacked up with the callers being interviewed by production staff to find the best callers. The banter between contestants and presenter may also be scripted. 'The producers hand-pick their contestants for personality, occupation and geographical spread as well as specialised knowledge, then arm themselves with a shrewd, thorough insight into the contestant's strength and weakness, and have full control of the questions he will be asked' ('The $60 Million Question', *Time*, www.time.com).

Channel 5 responded in January 2007 to Ofcom's paper on 'Participation TV' (you can view these official papers by going to the respective web sites). Channel 5 had *Quiz Call* late on Thursday, Friday and Saturday nights with editions shown on their digital channels. In their response to Ofcom's concerns Channel 5 stated that

'Quizzes and quiz-based programmes have always played a significant role in British television ... The new types of TV quiz shows are a further evolution of the quiz format. They differ from their predecessors in being based on viewers' participation via telephone and internet rather than on contestants in a studio. But they are still recognisably part of the same tradition – and as with all quizzes, viewers enjoy playing along at home without participating directly' (submission by Channel 5 Broadcasting Ltd. on Ofcom's issues paper on the regulation of 'Participation TV', January 2007).

In the paper Channel 5 also claimed that the suggestion by Ofcom that quiz TV programmes could be classified as teleshopping or advertising would 'simply mean the end of these programmes, and marginalisation of all such programmes onto dedicated and niche channels'. It suggested that the maximum time of advertising allowed by law of 12 minutes per hour on public service broadcasters like Channels 5 and 4 would make quizzes impossible to broadcast as by including them in their schedules they would go over the advertising limit (at the time of going to press, Ofcom was reviewing this regulation with a view to relaxing it).

See Activity 4i: Research the Industry's View

By May 2007 tough new rules had been introduced by the premium rate phones watchdog for TV quiz shows and channels. This resulted from the report by MPs who had been told of people spending thousands of pounds and practices that meant viewers were not being put through. Now viewers must be warned if they spend over £10 on phone calls and must be told how many others are taking part. In addition the price of calls must be read out every 10 minutes.

Phone-in quizzes are not unique to the United Kingdom. Telemedia InteractTV is a company that produces television quiz shows in 40 different countries. It is based in Budapest where all the programmes are produced. Young women of different nationalities are placed in front of screens representing the country to which they are broadcasting. Their job is to encourage viewers to phone in and play simple games. Depending upon the responses the producers will adjust the games and the prizes to maximize the number of calls and therefore profit. The studios run 24 hours a day. Local television companies run the shows with no overheads for them but with a share of the profits. The telephone companies also share in the profit from phone calls.

As well as the inserted local background, the control room adds music and sound effects such

NOTES:

as audience applause and drum rolls. The number of calls is monitored and to boost them the prize money seen on screen will be increased as the sound effects get louder. The show directors select a number of games from a pool. Some are based on local interests but most are simple puzzles and are not copyrighted. It is the analysis of what gets people to phone in, from the dress of the presenter to the size of prize, which is the key. When the directors think they have got the maximum calls for a game they will select callers until the right answer is given. The company pays out $1 million a month. Every country has different regulations and these are analysed before entering a country as, for example, Britain's laws on gambling. The US has strict laws: 'This is why we are entering the U.S. market only now where the regulation is the toughest' (Jeno Torocsik, founder of Telemedia InteractTV, Smith, www.nytimes.com, 20/11/2006).

4.9 Quiz Shows and Scandals

See Activity 4j: The Film *Quiz Show*

Quiz Show (1994, Robert Redford) looks at the quiz show scandal that rocked America in the 1950s over the quiz show *Twenty-One*. The tagline for the film is, 'Fifty million people watched, but no one saw a thing'. The quiz show producers had been feeding answers to the more attractive contestant, a WASP (white Anglo-Saxon protestant), in order to defeat the less attractive unpolished ex-GI, unappealing 'geek' from a Jewish ethnic background. This was because the sponsors of the show and the network owners wanted to use the winner for publicity and in 1950s America this meant a

certain (stereo)type of winner. The film shows how television worked and how 'men of money can rarely be reached for any wrong doing' (film review in www.imdb.com).

It showed how the producers coached the contestants to go through certain actions when they were under the spotlight as well as learn the answers.

Remember this is a dramatised account of the real events so do not use it for factual evidence. However, it does reveal how quiz shows (and other forms of television) can be manipulated. *Twenty One* was not the only US TV quiz show to be accused of rigging. *The $64,000 Question*, *Dotto* and *Tic Tac Dough* were others. (There is a further discussion of the events in several sources such as 'The Game Show' by Richard Goedkoop, in Rose, 1985.)

The quiz shows which followed offered smaller prizes and the emphasis shifted to celebrities and game like activities. These and the lower prize money quiz shows were profitable because of their low production costs and became the staple diet of daytime and early evening television in the United States (Goedkoop, in Rose, 1985). You can read more about the background to these quiz show scandals by using search engines such as Google if you type in 'quiz show scandals'.

However, it is not only the producers who may collude with contestants or weigh the chances of winning from one contestant to another. Contestants themselves can cheat without the knowledge of the producers.

In *Who Wants to be a Millionaire* (10 September 2001), a contestant won the million pound prize. It was said he had been helped by another contestant coughing at the right moment when he had to make a choice of answers. This led to the cancelling of the prize and a legal prosecution.

4.10 Conclusion

So firstly, the industry finds the format of the quiz show very profitable because it attracts audiences and is cheap to make. Secondly, institutional practices can limit the type of contestants through the working practices of the producers who want to provide entertainment (someone screaming ecstatically on the end of a phone is better entertainment than someone saying' thank you very much').

Finally the integration and convergence of different media have caused problems for regulators trying to control the processes as well as prizes.

Post-script

It does sound that the only winners of phone-in quizzes are the broadcasters. However I do know of someone who won a holiday to the Maldives and £10,000 by phoning in the correct answer to a breakfast show. Maybe you also know a lucky person – or you may even be one!

References

Aitkenhead, D. (1996) 'The Awful Allure of Phone-in TV' (Undercurrents), *New Statesman*, 25 Sept. 2006, InfoTrac OneFile Thomson Gale.

Dredge, S. (2007)'Crossed Lines. (Consumer TV Quiz Shows Flaws Exposed)', *New Media Age*, 19 April, InfoTrac OneFile, Thomson Gale.

'Minted; TV Quizzes. (Ethics of ITV Quiz Shows)', *The Economist* (US, 7 October 2006, InfoTrac OneFile, Thomson Gale.

Goedkoop, R., (1985) 'The Game Show', in Rose, B.C. (ed.) *TV Genres: A Handbook and Reference Guide*, London: Greenwood Press.

Smith, C. 'A Global TV Empire Built on Call-In Quiz Shows', in the *New York Times*, 20/11/2006.

Stone, J. and Yohn, T. (1992) *Prime Time Misdemeanors: Investigating the 1950s TV Quiz Scanda*, New Brunswick: Rutgers University Press.

Tedlow, R. (1976) 'Intellect on Television: The Quiz Show Scandals of the 1950s', *American Quarterly*, 28 (4): 483–95.

Turner, M. (2007)'Scandal Beats U.K. Quiz Channel: ITV Play Yanked as Phone-fee Scandal Hits B'casters', *Hollywood Reporter*, 398.36 March 14, p.4 (2) InfoTrac OneFile, Thomson Gale.

Wayne, M. (2000) '*Who Wants to be a Millionaire?* Contextual Analysis and the Endgame of Public Service Television', in Fleming, D. (ed.) *Formations: A 21st Century Media Studies Textbook*, Manchester: Manchester University Press.

Web sites

(www.en.wikipedia.org/Wiki/Quiz_Show)

www.library.digiguide.com/lib/category/ Has quiz shows listed and related links.

www.Ofcom.com

www.Channel5.co.uk

www.quiznite.co.uk/shows,asp with links to:

quizplayers.com – detailed background and material on a wide range of UK TV and Radio quizzes.

Memorable TV – brief details on hundreds of quiz and game shows from the 1950s to the present day part of the Memorable TV online encyclopaedia.

About The Human Internet – UKTV schedules.

NOTES:

Activity 4a: How many? Quantify

For a quick survey look at a television listings magazine and count up how many competition based shows are broadcast on terrestrial television over one month. You can do this by collecting a month's listings or by doing one week and multiplying the results by four. Your results may change with the seasons and the different schedules.

Activity 4b: Popularity

Audience Numbers: Now find out the weekly viewing statistics for quiz shows.

To do this go to www.barb.co.uk/viewingsummary/weekreports. BARB is the audience research bureau for broadcasters. It publishes regular statistics on audience viewing.

Choose the terrestrial channels first. Your results will depend upon both the year and the time of year you do this research. I did this in summer 2007 after there had been a controversy over phone-in competitions. The results for quiz shows in the top 30 programmes for 13/05/2007 were:

- BBC1 *Have I Got News For You* (11); *A Question of Sport* (26)
- BBC2 *Eggheads* (2; 10; 13; 19; 25) *The Weakest Link* (8; 18; 20; 21)
- ITV none
- Channel 4 none (although they had *Deal or No Deal*, a game show, in the following positions 5; 6; 7; 8; 9; 10)
- Channel 5 none

(N.B. The numbers in brackets show the position in the league table of audience size over a week.)

Now look at the statistics for Multi-Channel top 10. What results do you come up with?

These statistics should show you how important quiz (and game) shows are for channels.

Activity 4c: Audience

Look at the schedules for one day on terrestrial television. Can you see blocks of particular times? Would you be able to identify audiences from the genres (types) of programmes being broadcast? If you are working with a group you could each take one day and see if there were differences across different days. The weekend might be quite different to the weekday schedules, for example.

Broadcasters divide the day up into slots like this:

- Breakfast 6–9 a.m.
- The morning and afternoon 9 a.m.–4 p.m.
- Early evening or teatime 4–7 p.m.
- Primetime 7–11 p.m.
- Post-**watershed** 9 p.m.
- Night/overnight time 11 p.m.–6 a.m.

Activity 4d: Scheduling

This activity is made up of four parts:

1) Using your research in 4c state what types of programme are generally broadcast during these different periods. Where would you expect quiz shows to appear?

2) Each slot has a particular audience profile. In general who do you think would be the main target audience watching at each of the times above? (Work done in the audience section may help here.)

3) You are now going to do some **primary research** to find out what type of quiz shows are currently on during these slots and on which channel.

Just how many quiz shows are on television at the moment? This is quite a difficult question because with convergence the idea of television as a separate medium is becoming a little less obvious. We can now receive television through computer screens and even more mobile forms of communication. There are hundreds of different channels which add to the complexity of the (tele)visual world. For this activity we are going to stay with the traditional terrestrial channels which are still the main forms of general entertainment for the majority of viewers. This activity builds upon what you have already done above.

- Collect some TV listings magazines over several weeks (if possible from different times of the year as well).
- Look at the schedules.
- Write a chart with Monday to Sunday across the top.
- Mark the time periods listed above down the side.
- Now go through the schedules finding the quiz shows (be careful not to include game shows) being broadcast. Make a note of the channel. Do this for terrestrial television first.

If you have time you can also do a cable/satellite list as well.

4) From this primary research what general conclusions can you draw about the use of quiz shows in scheduling? Consider times, types of quiz programme, target audience, numbers of shows. For example, how many slots are given over to this type of programme in the prime time slot of early evening on terrestrial television? Which channels have the most quiz programmes? What does this evidence say about the use of quiz shows in scheduling?

Is there a slot when very few quiz shows are present?

Is there a difference between weekday and weekend quiz shows?

What is the most popular time?

Is there a difference between BBC and Commercial channels – ITV, Channel 4 and Channel 5?

Is there a commonality about any particular popular time slot for quiz shows?

What general changes do you notice from one time slot to another, for example, the type of questions or presenter?

What do these answers tell you about how the industry uses quiz shows?

Are there any quiz shows which stand out as popular and are shown maybe at a particular time slot like prime time (6–9 p.m.)? Are they different from the others? In what ways are they different?

You should now have a lot of information about how broadcasters use quiz shows to target audiences. Use this when you are constructing your own quiz shows.

Student Activities

Activity 4e: Lottery

What are 'lotteries'? How are they different from 'competitions'? Why should lotteries not be in favour with a broadcaster which had a public service ethos and which was paid for by the audience's licence money? (N.B. This question is not about the National Lottery show!)

Activity 4f: Rigged Competitions

One example of a rigged competition was when a TV quiz channel asked viewers to call, at a cost of 75p per call, to answer a question about what might be in a woman's handbag.

List what you think might be carried realistically in a handbag.

I might have included a purse/wallet, phone, handkerchief, pen, comb, etc.

In order to win a prize you *should* have included a balaclava, false teeth and Rawplugs (Dredge, 2007)!

Activity 4g: The Communication Line

Draw a horizontal line on a page; put "Broadcaster" at one end and "Audience" at the other. Who/what else will be in between? Put them on the line in the right position.

Broadcaster   Audience

●——●

(You could include: production company (like Celador and Hat Trick); schedulers; broadcasting company (like ITV); studio personnel such as presenters/editors/producers; the transmitting company (cable, satellite, terrestrial transmitters); the phone company; mobile network operators. At all these stages there could be errors.)

Activity 4h: Question

How would you get over the problem of the lines closing at midnight but your SMS message sent before midnight did not arrive because of technical delays until 00.02?

Student Activities

Activity 4i: Research the Industry's View

Do some research on broadcaster web sites and see if you can find their opinions on Ofcom's suggestions regarding 'Participation TV':

- www.bbc.co.uk

- www.channel4.co.uk

- www.itv.co.uk

- www.sky.co.uk

Activity 4j: The Film *Quiz Show*

If you have not already done so, watch *Quiz Show* (1994, Robert Redford).

'Cheating on a game show is like plagiarising a comic', Professor Van Doren, father of contestant played by Paul Schofield.

Having watched the film here are some discussion points to consider:

*   How truthful should non-fiction shows such as quiz and game shows be? Do you mind if they manipulate the truth for entertainment value?

*   Do you believe reality shows are 'rigged'? Is that a problem?

*   Does the look of contestants influence your feelings? (In the 1960s there was a famous debate between two candidates for the presidency of the USA Richard Nixon and Jack Kennedy. Those who watched on television said they would vote for Kennedy and those who listened on radio said they would vote for Nixon. Can you suggest why? If you can, have a look at photographs of the two men – you might even be able to watch a clip of the debate as it is often used to illustrate the point about the power of television. You will see that Nixon looks quite aged and tired whereas Kennedy looks young and healthy.)

*   Why should the way contestants look influence tension, drama and therefore ratings?

If you have watched the film, consider the following:

*   Do you feel that those involved in the quiz show were correctly motivated?

*   What power did each of the groups have?
    *   → The contestants.
    *   → The producers – 'The sponsors make out', 'Give the public what they want', 'It's entertainment'.
    *   → The Channel bosses – 'Television is a public trust' (chair of NBC).
    *   → The sponsors – 'They just wanted to watch the money'.
    *   → The politicians/judges.

Choose one of the people represented in the film from one of these groups. Write a defence of their actions and position regarding the quiz show. You could include, for example, their feelings towards others; what they gained or lost; what was their involvement in decision making; how much power they had; did they hurt anyone else through their decisions and actions.

Genre and Textual Analysis

5.1 Codes and Conventions

In analysing media texts a system known as **semiotics** (see Glossary) is often used. This is the 'science of signs' (de Saussure). For example, lighting and colour both signify. That is they are signs for ideas. So red is quite an aggressive colour connoting wars, fires, blood. But it can also connote romance, particularly if associated with a red rose or sexual availability if it is red lipstick. A red rose might also signify patriotism or regionalism. Semiotics looks at the micro detail; but we also look at the macro structures of genre and narrative to understand how meaning is constructed – or encoded by producers for audiences.

This section looks at these areas and contains several activities for textual analysis and primary research on the genre.

If you have read Section 2 you will know that the quiz show has shown great durability. Here we shall look at its generic formula and the changes that have developed within a changing media landscape.

Quiz shows are part of a genre of participation shows such as game shows and reality television where audiences are involved in the action, directly or indirectly. The basic element is Q and A but this may also appear in entertainment programmes where performing a task as well as answering questions is integral: a mixture of quiz and game show. Its flexibility as a form is seen when it becomes a pastiche celebrity quiz show such as *Never Mind the Buzzcocks*. The classic quiz show of questions and answers still appears durable and here we are keeping close to the question/answer format of the quiz show rather than the game format.

In both the Industries and Audiences sections we looked at the way channels have particular time slots for different audience profiles and broadcasting contexts. With a good formula the right quiz shows can attract audiences to less popular time slots such as after midnight with phone-ins (*Make Your Play*, ITV). In this section we are focusing on how the genre works for audiences and for producers through textual elements and iconography which help to identify and differentiate programmes.

Genre is a French word for 'type'. The general genre boxes that texts are put into such as science fiction and horror are not as clear cut as these names first appear. The quiz show for example is clearly part of the game show genre and can include elements of question and answer as well as 'play'. Quiz programmes have like other genres therefore been subject to genre-mixing.

The game show often has stunts and prizes for which no answers are necessary. They could be seen as part of the reality television shows where participants are also involved in game like activities. In its turn the reality show could be seen to be on the extreme edge of factual programmes such as documentaries by using a fly-on-the-wall style. So you can see there is a lot of slippage between genre 'boxes' and there may be different ways of approaching genre in order to reveal how audiences relate to texts (Hoerschelmann, 2006). For our definition a key factor in defining a quiz show appears to be (apparent) spontaneous answers.

How Do Quiz Shows Divide into Sub-genres?

- For the general public there are the money types of shows such as *Who Wants to be a Millionaire?* (ITV) and *The Weakest Link* (BBC2).

- At the other end of the spectrum there are the 'glory' shows for intellectual achievement such as *Mastermind* (BBC2), *University Challenge* (BBC2) and *Countdown* (C4).

- Finally, there are the cheaper quiz shows with minimal knowledge required which are often linked to home audience participation through phone-ins where a choice from possible answers can win prizes.

NOTES:

A variation on the quiz show is the personality/celebrity sub-genre such as *Have I Got News for You?* (BBC1), *Never Mind the Buzzcocks* (BBC2), *Schools Out* (BBC1), *QI* (BBC2) and *A Question of Sport* (BBC1). Here the questions and who wins are second to the entertainment provided by the celebrity teams and the presenter.

Sometimes there are hybrids of public/celebrity quizzes such as *Big Break*, which had a snooker player working with a contestant from the general public.

See Activity 5a: Watching Quiz Shows

When looking at this genre my students 'brainstormed' the quiz show genre and came up with this list of words. How far do you agree or disagree with them?

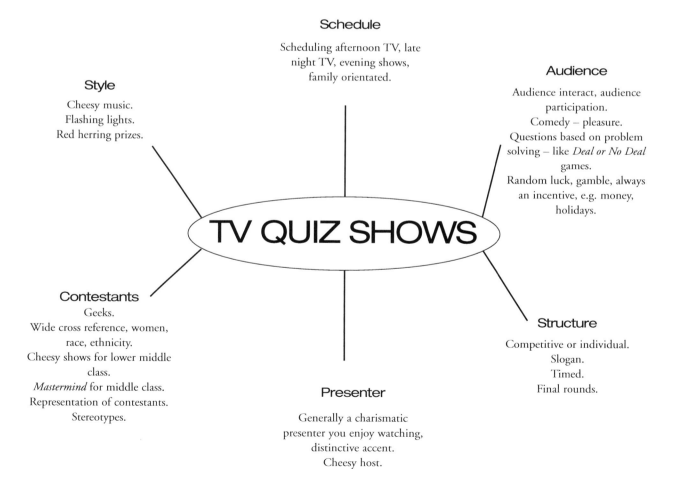

Schedule
Scheduling afternoon TV, late night TV, evening shows, family orientated.

Style
Cheesy music.
Flashing lights.
Red herring prizes.

Audience
Audience interact, audience participation.
Comedy – pleasure.
Questions based on problem solving – like *Deal or No Deal* games.
Random luck, gamble, always an incentive, e.g. money, holidays.

TV QUIZ SHOWS

Contestants
Geeks.
Wide cross reference, women, race, ethnicity.
Cheesy shows for lower middle class.
Mastermind for middle class.
Representation of contestants.
Stereotypes.

Presenter
Generally a charismatic presenter you enjoy watching, distinctive accent.
Cheesy host.

Structure
Competitive or individual.
Slogan.
Timed.
Final rounds.

Genre and Textual Analysis

5.2 Genre

There are several ways of approaching genre. The obvious one is to look at the textual similarities. In a quiz show these could include the following:

- The layout of the set.

- Camera use.

- Lighting and colour.

- *Mise-en-scène*.

- The use of particular types of 'characters'.

- The organisation of the rounds.

- The role of the presenter.

This similarity across different shows suggests a typicality of structure and content. There is, for example, a linear structure to the format. An introduction is followed by a series of rounds, each followed by a period of reflection/announcing scores/prize money won so far; followed by a ratcheting up of the tension to announce the winner and then a conclusion which may hook into the next round.

New quizzes reinvigorate the genre conventions whilst keeping the core code of question and answer. When a new format is successful then others will try to copy it. For example, *The Great Pretender* (ITV) broadcast in 2007 has similarities to BBC's *The Weakest Link*:

- The quiz show could be defined as a narrative in the sense that each person plays a role in the 'story'. These are hero, villain, helper, sender off on quest, blocker, false hero and goal (Propp). There is also an equilibrium/disequilibrium and new equilibrium within the structure (Todorov). Enigmas arise, such as how will a contestant react, and are answered (Barthes). There is a longer discussion of these narrative theories in Section 5.4.

Secondly, genre can also be studied as the product of a particular period reflecting changes in society. With the quiz show this is specifically attitudes to education, knowledge and to winning. So the differences between the kudos of being brain of Britain and the seemingly avariciousness of wanting to win a million is seen to reflect changes in social ideologies in Britain from the 1950s to the 1980s. The celebritisation of knowledge and the values that this implies are evident whether the contestant sits in a black chair, stands on a podium or in a booth. This trend towards the celebritisation of popular culture, which some claim is seeping into public areas of society, is perhaps signified in the size of the prizes on offer. The desire to win large sums of money without work is evident in other areas such as the Lotto.

In America a trend from authoritarian quizzes to audience participation games was said to reflect changes in that society. Apparently there was a sign in an office that stated 'You can learn more about America by watching a half-hour of "Let's Make a Deal" than you can from watching Walter Cronkite for a month' (Goedkoop in Rose, 1984, p.296). Cronkite was an eminent news journalist and commentator on society.

Thirdly, genres can be seen to reflect technological, industrial and social change. Technology has influenced the way quiz shows are now consumed as convergence and the digital world allow us to use this new technology to be more interactive as audiences. Whether you regard technology as constructing new ways of thinking and interacting with the media, as with the theory of **technological determinism** (Raymond Williams, 1974) or whether you believe society's demands form the basis of how technology is used (such as the way we use texting on phones), there is still an effect in the way we interact with the new forms. The demand for profitable entertainment as television combats the digital world could be seen to influence the way that quiz programmes are used to attract audiences. Each show has to differentiate itself from others so as to find new ways of targeting audiences and therefore will introduce new elements as well as retaining tried and tested formula. New technology helps to provide these changes, for example, the ability to

NOTES:

'ring a friend' in *Millionaire* was a result of technological innovation.

Genres can also be approached through the different types of pleasure given to audiences. The psychology of the audience and the way we identify with contestants. Audiences and their interest in playing along with contestants is an important factor for the genre. Our pleasures in watching winners and losers and the streak of the chancer in all of us, are satisfied by the quiz show. Will the right questions come up for us? Will we be quick enough? We participate vicariously and we enjoy the thrill and tension of the scene on the screen, without losing face if we cannot answer, but with a warm glow of self-satisfaction if we get it right.

Finally, genres can be approached in an historical way by looking at how, through a combination of factors, genres can be seen to change and develop. They move through an experimental stage where elements are tried out. The successful ones then use the tried and tested format moving into the classic stage. This moves into a reflective stage, where the format becomes self-referential, as with *QI*, and finally into a period of decline before new approaches may create a revival. At all points of this development the genre can be targeted for parody and pastiche.

Using these broad approaches of text, producers, audience and changes through time we are going to investigate how the quiz show works as a genre.

5.3 Expectations and Definitions

As indicated earlier the quiz show has a number of sub-genres ranging from the intellectual such as *Mastermind* to the simple breakfast programme style quizzes where viewers phone/text choosing one of three answers and go into a lucky dip draw.

The basic Q and A format needs refining for each new quiz by testing with audiences and participants. Good ideas are not enough. According to folklore the idea for *Mastermind* with the black chair and spotlight came from its creator's experience of interrogation in a prisoner of war camp – name, number and rank. This was used in the opening sequence (name, occupation and specialist topic) and set the tone for the rest of the successful format.

5.4 The Medium – Television

It is important to remember that each medium has different characteristics and are more suited to some types of text than others. So before looking at the characteristics of a quiz show in more detail think first about the medium it is in because that will influence its style and form.

Whatever we see on television has been 'mediated'. It has gone through a range of choices made by others before we choose to switch on and view. This means it is highly constructed and does not represent reality but only a view of the real world. We are being presented with images chosen by others who have their own agenda and institutional practices. These images in mass media such as television are read by large numbers and this is why the media are seen to be powerful conveyers of messages. So what techniques are used to do this re-presentation? What are television's special characteristics?

The elements that make up television as a medium include the following:

- It is a domestic medium.

- It has a small screen.

- It uses audio and visual moving images with graphics.

- All the material is edited.

- It has technical constraints such as camera framing and lighting.

- There are institutional constraints such as regulation, both self, such as the watershed agreement for 9 p.m, and statutory, as with the BBC Trust and Ofcom, as well as the laws of the land.

- Terrestrial television still targets a mass audience although this is gradually shrinking.

Television has its own language. Quiz shows are generally produced in studios (*Mastermind* is an exception being filmed on location). This means artificial lights, static sets, formulaic camera shots and editing style.

Particular camera positions are used to frame close-up and two shots (where two people are in the frame). Generally wide and long shots are less used in television studio shows. Close-ups are more frequently used because of the size of the studio, the size of the domestic screen and because the audience want to see the reaction on the faces of the contestants. Shot reverse shot is commonly used in dialogue. Think about how a conversation is normally filmed in a soap opera, for example. (If you are not sure about the technical codes of television there are many media introductory books and web sites which give a brief rundown of these, such as www.mediaknowall.com and www.mediaed.org. The BFI have also produced a good introduction to film language CD-Rom or look at www.screenonline.com.)

Genre and Textual Analysis

A studio set up means cameras have to be carefully positioned so they are not seen by the viewing audience. Cameras can sometimes be 'hand held' using a steadicam to get among the studio audience or one can sweep over the audience to add excitement and intensity. This is done particularly at the opening of the show or between rounds.

Although cameras can pan, zoom and tilt, in a quiz studio the movement is more likely to be through cutting from one camera to another; that is in camera editing. The cameras are generally on eye level so we are positioned as observers. Cameras are placed in positions to look at the contestants, the presenter and sometimes the studio audience to increase the tension in what is often a very static set-up. Techniques such as the close-ups of contestants concentrating on answering the question build suspense. Editing is usually straight cuts rather than special dissolves and fades. An editor selects the order of shots to create meaning to convey the 'narrative' of the show. They may, for example, cut in several shots of a participant seen to be under stress in order to build suspense and drama. Editing will be done by the producer and then fine tuned afterwards before being broadcast. Even in a programme like *Big Brother* which appears 'live' and 'real' there are several editors looking at different cameras and these are controlled by a 'master' editor who decides which camera to go to. (After the accusations of racist comments by Jade Goodey, Channel 4 who commissioned this show, have been even more editor conscious.)

Lighting and colour are also part of the technical codes which create meaning and are linked to the type of quiz show. *Mastermind*, for example, has a spotlight on the black leather and steel chair for the contestant and the desk of the questioner/interrogator. The rest of the studio is darkened. This adds to the combatant feel and tension. Other quiz shows have high key lighting to create an everyday feel which connotes that ordinary people are taking part or to create a buzzy atmosphere. In *The Weakest Link* the audience are asked to wear dark clothes to maintain the overall coolish colour tones.

Although most quizzes are based upon dialogue sound helps to create atmosphere and meaning such as non-diegetic music with diegetic sound effects sounds such as bells and beepers to indicate an answer is to be given – 'first to the buzzer'. The signature tune is important as it highlights the type of show through the rhythm and instrumentation and indicates to an audience that the programme is beginning. This can become an iconic element of the show. The classic one is *Mastermind*. As the cameras zoom into the empty black chair, the sound track of ominous and portentous drums sound. The gladiatorial nature of the set is therefore reflected in the music. Sometimes there is a musical motif which indicates an end of a round or as in *Countdown* a clock indicates time ticking away. Background music is generally not used during the Q and A as speech is privileged.

See Activity 5b: Sound and Camera Positions

One important point about genre is that there is always a tension between the old formula and innovation to excite an established audience or target a new audience.

Audiences will generally want to have an idea of the type of programme they are watching. The programme's promotion through listings, reviews and trailers will have raised their awareness and expectation. The use of inheritance, pre-echo, hammocking and common junction points will have all been used to attract, capture and maintain the audience (see Section 4 Industries and Institutions).

5.5 Genre and Narrative

The way that stories are told is linked directly to the genre in which it is set. Consider how a detective story keeps you guessing about the

NOTES:

perpetrator of the crime whilst a thriller lets you know who it is so that you can follow the chase. Narrative theories can be applied to the quiz show. Again you can find out more about these in general media books such as Branston and Stafford's *Media Students Book* (2007). You may not think a quiz show has a narrative or a plot but let's consider how such a show is structured.

We can apply Todorov's theory of narrative based upon equilibrium and agent of change. There is an opening which establishes the protagonists – the contestants and presenter, the initial equilibrium. There is the challenge they face which creates the disruption and the rest of the show, the disequilibrium is dealing with this challenge. The closure and new equilibrium provide us with the winner and of course the losers. In addition there are opening and closing title sequences and credits to mark the boundaries of the narrative/**diegesis**.

Vladimir Propp looked at stories, particularly folk and fairy stories, and their similarities and suggested various commonalities such as the steps through which narratives move, the role of characters and the use of tripling devices. The participants play roles, such as the dispatcher, the helper, the blocker, the villain, the prize and the hero. So the presenter is the dispatcher of the contestants off on a quest. A helper may be the 'friend' they ring or the presenter may also help, particularly in a celebrity show where winning is not the whole prize. The blocker will be the other participants/team. The villain again may be played by the presenter such as Anne Robinson or another participant. The hero will be the winner and their goal is the prize.

Psychologists who have studied the quiz show suggested that the popularity of them can be attributed to the narrative structure which they say resembles ancient myths and fairy tales. They suggest that the audience 'may gain satisfaction from the playing out of an evolutionarily significant behaviour sequence in which the hunter becomes heroic' (Roiser and Stevens, 2001).

As with fairy stories such as 'Jack and the Beanstalk' the contestants have to climb a ladder of increasingly difficult and dangerous steps to reach the golden 'egg', getting help from the audience, or a friend, or the team, or the host, but these are possible false helpers like the sirens of ancient myths. Do you think it is possible to describe a quiz show in terms of a fairy story or myth?

Roland Barthes, a media theorist, discussed five codes which he said could be used to do an analysis in micro terms of a narrative. Briefly these are the action and enigma codes such as the

use of questions and answers to move the meaning along (primary) and the cultural, symbolic and semic (secondary) codes. The latter include the dress codes, the non-verbal communication of the participants, the use of lighting and colour to symbolise ideas and so on. For example, we could see the Anne Robinson persona dressed in long black clothes as signifying various cultural references.

So quiz shows 'contain conflict, rising interest, a climax, and a denouement' (in Mittell, 2004, pp.29-55).

5.6 Format

Inside the diegesis there is a pattern in the structure of the show which fans particularly will know and will expect to see. For example, there may be narrative cues of a particular shot or an announcement of the next round.

We can divide these expectations into a structure such as:

- The set.

- The personalilty/presenter often with a catchphrase.

- The contestants – general public and/or celebrities.

- The prizes.

- A live audience or 'canned'.

- Glamour sometimes associated with a female assistant.

- Excitement associated with competition.

My typography of quiz shows would also include:

- Title's connotations.

- Channel.

- Scheduling.

- Audience – home/studio.

- Questions – type whether easy, hard, intellectual, general, specific.

We will look at some of these in more detail.

Genre and Textual Analysis

5.7 The Set

See Activity 5c: Analysis of a TV Quiz Show Set

Each quiz show has its own style but the layout is often quite similar. The basic concept is to have a challenge between teams or contestant with a questioner. If it is the questioner and the contestant they may be positioned so that they are facing each other in a sort of gladiatorial spectacle. Other contestants may sit in a line to show equality at the beginning. In a team quiz the opposition between the teams may be signified by being placed on either side of the questioner. This could also be a sign for the neutrality of the questioner, rather like a referee at the beginning of a match. The contestant and presenters will usually sit/stand behind a desk/table. Mostly head and shoulders are visible rather than legs. Why should this be so? Occasionally contestants/presenters will come from behind their desks or they may be in full view as with *The Weakest Link* where they stand in a semi-circle. *The Weakest Link* has a semi-circular layout that reflects the title, but why should the contestants stand rather than sit?

To increase the atmosphere sets are made exciting with lights and colour. The context is all important. Dramatic lighting, such as **chiaroscuro** with strong dark shadows and bright lit pools could connote conflict. Does it reference other genres? Consider how in a police drama, or in a film noir detective story, or any similar situation the interviewer and interviewee are presented in pools of light across a table with the background in total shadow. By using these signifiers the set designer will hope to pull on these cultural knowledges to read conflict in the quiz show. The colours in quiz shows tend to be cool blue/silver. Angles are sharp and surfaces reflective. What does this signify?

Consider the cost of the sets. Do you think they are expensive? Do you see the same set each week? In some quiz shows the ultimate winner from several contestants may have the opportunity of winning a mega prize. If this happens the contestant is often taken to a different point in the set. Here the lighting and positioning will emphasise their isolation – such as with a spotlight from above and with the studio lights dimmed.

5.8 The Presenters

Not only the contestants can be selected using particular types but this accusation could also be levelled against the presenters. The American quiz show of the latter half of the twentieth century was seen to be dominated by male quizmasters: 'The amiable, attractive, masculine host is as essential a part of the fantasy as the payoff…there is no quiz or game show that has successfully installed a female host; [he] is the romantic element common to all these shows' (Goedkoop, in Rose, 1984, p.298).

Note the date of this publication and consider if this is still true.

See Activity 5d: Presenters

The presenter is often the key to the success of a quiz. Most presenters are in there for the long term. When they leave, it is often newsworthy. *Have I Got News for You* suddenly lost Angus Deayton as the eponymous straight faced presenter fielding the humour of Paul Merton and Ian Hislop. This was as a result of Deayton becoming a news item and as a result the butt of jokes. Instead of replacing Deayton directly the producers have tried out a range of celebrity figures. Can you name other quizzes where the presenter left and was replaced? Who replaced them? Why do you think they were chosen as replacements?

Replacing a well known face is often quite tricky even for established personalities. For example, Des O'Connor took over *Countdown* Channel 4's 'flagship quiz show'. A newspaper report suggested that "Des O'Connor was being partly blamed yesterday for a fall in Channel 4 viewing figures. The channel lost 10 percent of its

NOTES:

audience share in the first half of 2007 compared to the same period last year according to the official industry body, Barb' (Pettie, 'Countdown to Disaster for Des', *Daily Telegraph*, 3 July 2007).

There are a number of other questions you can ask about the presenters.

Consider how a presenter enters the set. Are they already present or do they appear?

Look at the NVC (non-verbal communication) of the presenter. Analyse their dress, hair, actions and voice. Do they have a catchphrase? What is their style? Is it friendly, jokey, abrasive? Is there any difference between male and female presenters?

What does the look and style of the presenter tell us about the type of quiz show it is?

What do the other jobs the presenter has in the media effect their role in the quiz show? Consider, for example, Sue Barker who was an important British tennis player; and who has successfully chaired a *Question of Sport*. She is also a presenter at sports events such as Wimbledon. Does the presenter indicate the target audience of the quiz show? For example, *A Question of Sport* originally had a male presenter and the contestants are usually male. What does Sue Barker bring to the role?

Presenters often develop catchphrases which can enter into general usage.

Here are some catchphrases:

*   I've started so I'll finish – *Mastermind*.
*   I don't want to give you that – *Millionaire*.
*   The higher they go the bigger the dough – *Wipeout*.
*   Phone a friend – *Millionaire*.
*   Is that your final answer? – *Millionaire*.
*   You are the weakest link, goodbye – *The Weakest Link*.

5.9 The Contestant

As there are different types of presenter so there are different groups of contestants.

Firstly, there is the celebrity contestant and team who get paid or who may donate their winnings to a charity as with *School's Out* (BBC1). Secondly, there are the ordinary public who volunteer for the show, often in the hope of winning a prize. These people will register with web sites or will put themselves forward to go through selection processes of a particular

programme. Thirdly, there is a combination of ordinary person and celebrity, for example, in *Big Break* (BBC).

What qualities do you consider make a good contestant? Here are some suggested by Liz Roberts ('Deal or No Deal and the TV game show' in *Media Education Journal* 40, pp.20-25). These were for game shows, but the same criteria may apply to quiz shows:

*   A good sport – win or lose.
*   Have some (amateur) talent even if not a celebrity.
*   Must not be unattractive.
*   Must not be in need.
*   Must not cheat.

Do you agree with her?

See Activity 5e: Contestants

If you can, view the film *Quiz Show* (1994, Robert Redford). One of the reasons this was such a scandal in the States was the way that apparently the contestants were specifically chosen for their ethnicity and looks.

It is interesting to find out how the contestants are chosen. For example, for *Raise the Roof* for which the prize was a house, there were open auditions conducted in nine cities around the UK with 20,000 applicants. An initial general knowledge test was followed by a personality test in which applicants had to talk about themselves to the assembled company. From this group around 60 were recalled for a second audition. There was another general knowledge paper overseen by invigilators and a questionnaire asking questions such as what their 'party piece' was (Lock, 'Game for a laugh?' *Radio Times*, pp.26-7).

You can find out more about putting yourself forward for quizzes by visiting web sites, such as www.beonscreen.com/uk/user/all-game-show-quiz-shows.asp.

Like the presenter, the celebrity contestants tend to have a role to play, either the 'let's have a laugh', the 'straight faced' one, the 'fast quipper', the 'exuberant' one and so on. If you can watch a show with celebrities and suggest the type of role they perform in the show.

5.10 The Audience
The Studio Audience

Some quiz shows have a studio audience to watch or even to participate and to be the stand in or surrogate for the audience at home, reflecting the tension for the home audience's

Genre and Textual Analysis

enjoyment. The immediate studio audience is small. If you live near a recording studio you may be able to attend a recording session although some times there is an age limit. The audience often contain friends/families of the contestants, clubs and groups on outings, and people who have an interest in television production such as media students and who are there to see how a show is put together. In addition there will be fans of the show or the celebrities involved.

Some shows have a very committed following and have a cult status. For example, on radio there is a programme called *I'm Sorry I Haven't a Clue* which was hosted until his death in 2008 by the veteran jazz musician Humphrey Littleton. This attracts packed out audiences in large venues across the country. As a radio show it does not need a special studio set up. But on stage it is still set out as two teams sitting opposite each other with the question master in the centre. It plays with the listening audience in a self-knowing way. For example the presenter, Littleton, referred to his assistant 'Samantha', who is described as an attractive young woman with many sexual innuendoes attached to her. In fact there is no Samantha and the nearest person to an assistant for Humph was a male producer. Another in-joke is the fact that in spite of what is told to the radio audience there is no hi-tech screen showing the audience the answer the teams have to guess, but a piece of cardboard held aloft by the 'assistant'.

What is required of the studio audience?

If you have ever been to a TV recording as an audience you will know that often there is a warm up comic to get the audience laughing and 'loosened or warmed up'. There is also a floor manager who gets the audience clapping at the required points in the show. The audience may be rehearsed into certain actions or responses for the show. Certain cameras will be used to cut to the audience for reaction shots or as cutaways used, for example, between rounds. The audience therefore helps with the atmosphere.

See Activity 5f: Audiences

5.11 The Prizes

Prizes in quiz shows can be cash, sometimes consumer goods and sometimes just the glory. *Mastermind* gives no consolation prizes just the chance to go on to the next round. The final 'mastermind' will get a piece of art or similar prize of relatively little monetary value. In 2008 it was an engraved glass bowl. The larger prize money quizzes however becomes a way for the winner to achieve a goal, which is often quite limited, such as a holiday. It is only a very few that have prizes which are life-changing such as winning a million pounds would be. Those quiz shows which provide commodities such as cars may provide 'free' advertising space for the manufacturer.

Some shows have built a reputation on huge prizes but even the smaller ones are met with ecstatic reactions by audiences and contestants. The excitement that is generated by the presenter and the studio audience, partly through the use of technical codes can build up the winning amount to seem extraordinary. Fiske suggests that this can relate to the idea of '**jouissance**' (a word used by Roland Barthes to suggest a particular type of over-the-top or extreme pleasure. The other more regular pleasure Barthes called **plaisir**).

5.12 Titles

NOTES:

Titles are important because they often indicate the style of show or its main organising factor. They encapsulate the type of quiz show. Their words connote certain attributes. Like images words have symbolic and cultural meanings. They also connect with ideologies or beliefs about society. Many titles will connect with meanings from other sources; that is, they have cultural significance or **intertextual** references. They use well known phrases such as 'the weakest link' in a chain, or 'countdown' or 'top of the form'. The phrase 'who wants to be a millionaire' comes from a famous popular song written by Cole Porter and sung in the film *High Society* (1956).

Other titles will suggest the type of quiz show involved. Can you guess the format from the title *Take It or Leave It* which was the original title of *The $64,000 Question* quiz when it was first on radio? Does it suggest a similar format in contemporary British television?

See Activity 5g: Titles

See Activity 5h: Title Sequence

See Activity 5i: Extension Activity on Title Sequence

5.14 Conclusion

The formula of the quiz show is basically quite simple, but even so there are differences of style and content which provide variety to appeal to different audiences. The quiz show as a genre and its development through time also tell us much about the values society attaches to such things as knowledge and entertainment as well as money. The essential element is of the potential for being lifted out of the mundane real world into the colourful, exotic, exciting world of the quiz game. In the debates section these issues will be looked at in more detail.

References

Barthes, R. (1972) *Mythologies*, London: Cape.

Branston, G. and Stafford, R. (2007) *Media Students Book*, 4th edn, London: Routledge.

Goedkoop, R. (1984) 'The Game Show', in Rose, B.C. (ed.) *TV Genres: A Handbook and Reference Guide*, London: Greenwood.

Hoerschelmann, O. (2006) *Rules of the Game: Quiz Shows and American Culture*, New York: SUNY Press.

Pettie, A. 'Countdown to Disaster for Des', *Daily Telegraph*, 3 July 2007.

Propp, V. I. (1968) *Morphology of the Folk Tale*, Texas: Austin University of Texas Press.

Roiser, M. and Stevens, D. (2001) 'The Mythic Nature of a Quiz Show Turf Wars, and the Sex Life of the Japanese Earwig', *The Chronicle of Higher Education*, Vol.48 (11), 9 Nov.

Todorov, T. (1977) 'The Grammar of Narrative' in *The Poetics of Prose*, New York: Cornell University Press.

Williams, R. (1974) *Media, Technology and Society*, London: Fontana.

Student Activities

Activity 5a: Watching Quiz Shows

You may already have a list of quiz shows; if not, compile one below.

What quiz shows do you watch? Make a list. Compare the list with others. Is there any disagreement about what is or isn't a quiz show? Why did this occur?

From this list can you create the elements you would say are essential for a quiz show? Again make a list and compare with others. Could you draw up a typography of the genre of quiz show?

Activity 5b: Sound and Camera Positions

Camera Positions

- Watch part of a quiz show that you have recorded. Note down what types of camera work has been used. You could use words like pan, tilt, track, close-up, medium shot, long shot, moving shot.

- Watch again and look at the lighting and colours. Consider words such as spotlight, backlight, silhouette, fill light, high or low key lighting, cool or warm colours.

- Watch a third time and note the types of editing being used.

Sound

Listen to a range of signature tunes without the visuals. What do these convey aurally? Can you tell what types of instruments are used? Is there a particular style in general for quiz signature tunes?

Student Activities

Activity 5c: Analysis of a TV Quiz Show Set
Consider one quiz show with which you are familiar.

Draw a plan of the set as though you were looking down on it from above – a bird's eye view.

Label each of the elements. These might include:

- Presenter's chair/desk.
- Presenter's helper.
- Contestant's chair/desk.
- Audience blocks – there may be more than one – why is this so?
- Other contestants or teams.
- Possible camera positions.
- Background screens hiding the behind the scenes activities, such as contestants waiting or coming off to be interviewed about their experience.

If some in your group have done other quiz shows you can compare them.

In general what similarities/differences are there?

Can you make generalised statements about the sets for such shows?

For example, what type of background is used? Is it elaborate or simple? Do you think it was expensive?

Do the contestants and presenter stay in the same relative positions?

Are any other spaces used? If so, what is their purpose?

Do you think the title is reflected in the set?

Consider the lighting and colours used. How do they help to create meaning?

Do the background and layout (*mise-en-scène*) reflect the type of quiz and its themes?

Activity 5d: Presenters

Draw up a list of presenters (you may already have a list from a previous activity).

What type or style do you consider each of the presenters represents? Write the names of quiz presenters against the style you think they are most like:

- The teacher.
- The teaser.
- The joker.
- The inquisitor.
- The cruel one.
- The kindly helper.
- The master.

How does the style of the presenter reflect the type of quiz show?

Can you make any other general statements about the presenters? For example, do they have other roles in the media? How long have they been around the media world – are they new to it or not? Are they male or female in general? Are they young or old?

Would the presenters work in other quiz scenarios. For example, could Des O'Connor present *University Challenge*? Remember all he has to do is read out questions which is what he does in *Countdown*. Do the qualities of each presenter transfer to other genres? For example, could a soap star become a presenter? In which other genre do you think the presenter would be able to work? Does this list help to define the qualities of the presenter which make them successful in a quiz show? What are these qualities? (Keep these answers and ideas for quick reference when you are devising your own quiz show.)

Extension Activity

Watch an extract from a quiz show with a strong presenter such as *The Weakest Link*:

- Write down any thoughts about persona.
- Comment on dress, hair, facial expressions, actions.
- Consider the type of language used (words and sentence structures) and the mode of address (how they talk to the competitors).
- Now look at the technical codes of lighting, camera angle, sound, editing, colours. Is there anything in the design which helps to enhance this persona?

Student Activities

Activity 5e: Contestants

If you have watched the film *Quiz Show* you can compare your research with how the contestants are represented in the film.

Look at your list of quiz shows. Choose one where the general public are the contestants. Think of the show and the type of contestants that generally appear.

Consider the following:

- Age.
- Gender.
- Dress code.
- Accents/dialects.
- Class.
- Race and ethnicity.
- Interests and background, e.g. occupation.

Do they have an image or general persona that you can identify? Could you describe a typical contestant in the show?

Is this why they have been chosen? For example, are they a bit quirky or are they ordinary – would you walk past them in the street? What does each type bring to the show?

Are there contestants that you think have been particularly chosen? Does this suggest a selection not on ability but on other criteria?

Are there any contestants who are bit out of the 'ordinary' – maybe wearing a different style of dress or hairstyle, perhaps someone in a wheelchair? If you can spot something different comment on what it says about that particular show and what effect it has on the meaning of the show. My students said that they had noted that *The Weakest Link* had a range of different types of contestant. Could you give a reason why this might be so?

Activity 5f: Audiences

Using earlier work on television codes watch a section of a quiz show that is recorded with an audience present and work out how the audience is presented through camera and editing. How much do you see of the audience?

- Look at the audience make up. For example, is it predominantly of a particular age group or gender? Are there any other similarities?
- Does the studio audience help you in identifying the target audience sitting at home?

Why do quiz shows often have studio audiences? Is it to provide a livelier atmosphere for the participants or is it to provide a response to the presenters' quips? Can you think of any other reasons?

What quiz shows do *not* have studio audiences? Why not? Is it because the show is on so often it would not be possible to get a studio audience regularly? Is it because the presenter is not an audience entertainer? What other reasons could there be?

Student Activities

Activity 5g: Titles

If you have already written down a list of quiz show titles to what cultural knowledge do they link? (**Connotation** means what each title suggests or implies.) For example:

Mastermind connotes that the winner will be the best, the cleverest person.

Countdown connotes ....

Activity 5h: Title Sequence

The title sequence will be used every time the show appears and represents its identity.

The title sequence also helps to confirm the style of the show. Look at the title sequence of several contemporary quiz shows. Analyse the sequences using all the elements such as lighting, colour, sound, camera, editing, graphics of the title sequence.

Title	Lighting/Colour	Sound	Camera	Editing	Graphics

Does the title sequence remind you of other genres?

Is it simple or complex?

What does it say about the quiz show?

You can repeat this several times and note similarities and differences.

Activity 5i: Extension Activity on Titles

Here are some quiz show titles. Some you will know but many probably not. What are the types of shows suggested by, and the connotations, of these titles? Give reasons for your answers and try to use media terms such as connotation, target audience, signify, ideology.

For example, to me *Have a Go* suggests quite an amateurish approach. It's the sort of phrase you would use with friends, for example, in a funfair at the hoopla stall. It's a well used colloquialism or phrase (cultural knowledge) – 'go on have a go' – and there seems to be a subtext which adds 'it doesn't matter if you fail, it's all in good fun. We're on your side (identification) because we would be just as bad/good as you are'. So the target audience feels that it is ordinary people and the message is that *you* can be a winner – just have a go, even if you come from ordinary stock (ideology).

Title	Connotations	Cultural References	Audience
Ask Me Another			
What's My Line?			
Animal, Vegetable or Mineral			
Top of the Form			
Brain of Britain			
Double Your money			
Take Your Pick			
Criss Cross Quiz			
Countdown			
Mastermind			
Wheel of Fortune			
Beat the Clock			
University Challenge			
Celebrity Squares			
Face the Music			
Give Us a Clue			
Chance of a Lifetime			
Hit the Jackpot			

Case Studies

Introduction

In the genre/textual analysis section we saw how quiz shows follow a formula of question and answer with variables such as types of question and style of presenter. In this section we are going to look in more detail at some of the most popular television quiz programmes. Interestingly, in general, the longer running series have been those that have not offered big prizes.

6.1 The Formula

As we have seen in the genre section the formula includes elements such as:

- The layout of the set.

- The prizes.

- The presenter.

- The camera style and lighting.

- The 'rounds'.

- The types of question.

- The type of teams/individuals.

- The use of voice over, buzzers.

- Time constraints.

Once established the structure tends to stay the same. The only elements that usually change from programme to programme are the questions and contestants. In terms of new quizzes innovation occurs such as the ability to have phone-ins and for the home audience to participate on-line as in *Test the Nation*. But in general the formula remains little changed.

The differences between quizzes are associated with the audience appeal and the technical codes which help to create meaning for audiences. These include lighting and colour, camera, editing, *mise-en-scène*, sound and so on. This section looks more closely at these elements through specific case studies.

6.2 *The Weakest Link* (BBC August 2000–present)

The Weakest Link is hosted by Anne Robinson who has made her sharp retorts and signature wink the brand of this programme: 'it has won plaudits and opprobrium in equal measure, garnering unlikely enemies such as mastermind host Magnus Magnusson, who has described the show as a "theatre of cruelty", and commentator Ludovic Kennedy, who labelled it "trash"' (Knight, *Sunday Express*, 4 March 2001).

The show was devised to create a quiz that had all the best bits from other general knowledge shows such as *University Challenge* with its irascible presenter, who is (to date) Jeremy Paxton, but with an element of the gladiatorial as well. *The Weakest Link* goes out on the BBC2 teatime slot, a popular time for these programmes (see the research on the Industries, Section 4). Why is this type of programme popular at tea-time? Consider the **demographics** of the audiences at this time. Do the audience have a similar profile to the participants?

When it was first broadcast *The Weakest Link* became the best rating show for BBC2 with 5 million viewers regularly watching it at 5.15 p.m. BBC1 then held a 'champion's league' in prime time which attracted another 3 million viewers. The show was immediately sold to NBC (a national network) in America where the prize was raised to $1million, and it has now 'gone global'.

NOTES:

It has become one of the BBC's most successful exports (Knight, 2001).

The title is significant. We know culturally that there is a saying about someone being the weakest link in a chain of events and that a chain is only as strong as its weakest link. The title therefore uses this audience cultural knowledge as well as reflecting how the show works. The graphics of the title appears each time the 'weakest link', that is, one of the players, is voted off re-affirming the meaning of the title. The circularity of the meaning of the words, i.e. the links of a chain are symbolically represented in the visual layout of the set and the way Anne Robinson the presenter swivels around addressing each of the eight contestants (the links in the chain) in turn.

Contestants work as a team to accumulate prize money. This is quite substantial for a BBC programme with the possibility of currently winning up to £10,000. (Remember what was said about public service broadcasting and how its ethos did not match with large prizes – see Section 4.) After each round the 'worst' or weakest contestant is voted out by the team until there are two left to fight individually for the money that has been accumulated.

At each round there is a brief interview with the contestants about their choice for ejection. Here there is gamesmanship at work as a contestant might want to vote off a stronger member of the 'team' if they think they would have a better chance at the end of taking the accumulated money against a weaker opponent. When the contestants vote off the weakest link they have to write the name on a board and give their reasons for their choice which accentuates the personal element. The rounds are commented upon by a male voice over who before the contestants vote releases the actual facts about who answered most and least questions and who is therefore statistically the weakest link.

The ejected contestants give their response to camera in a separate studio booth.

The format therefore combines the cerebral element of knowledge with voyeuristic pleasures that are part of the type of pleasures usually associated with reality shows and gamesmanship.

The presenter Anne Robinson is often dressed in long black clothes with spiky shoes. She looks and behaves like a dominatrix hitting the contestants with verbal strikes. There are calculated rude remarks such as, 'What did you learn at school?' But Robinson smiles at the beginning and end of the show (the element of ritual that Fiske, 1987, discusses), where she also gives her trade-mark wink which suggests that

everything that has gone before including her rudeness is defused – although not too much. In America where the audience started to laugh at her cruel quips they were asked not to as this spoilt the 'Cruella' image of Robinson. This rudeness does not put off people wanting to be on the show and at one point the BBC had to stop advertising for contestants.

The programme differentiates itself from other quizzes by the persona of Anne Robinson who is not only female but is also in many ways the opposite to other hosts where the prizes are substantial. Usually the host is kind and commiserates with the losers. Anne is antagonistic and rude.

The contestants are picked at random, interviewed and then trialled to see that they do not crumble under the Robinson remarks. The contestants appear to want to spar with Robinson and that is part of the appeal of the show: '…the appeal is waiting to see what Anne's going to do next' (cameraman on show, in Knight, 2001).

See Activity 6a: Discussion

The afternoon audience in the studio is made up of students, housewives, the unemployed, older people, all of whom are representative of the fan-base. They are told to wear dark clothes to help maintain the darker tones of the show. The set is bathed in blue tones and with spotlights. It has a cold clinical feel to it.

The studio set is a semi-circle with Robinson in the centre. Each contestant has a podium at which they stand, as does Anne with the questions in front of her. The signature music and motifs are synthetic and abrupt and have a sharp staccato emphasis rather like Robinson's heels.

See Activity 6b: Persona

Case Studies

6.3 *Mastermind* (BBC1 1972–97 hosted by Magnus Magnusson; revived in 2003–present with John Humphries as quizmaster)

Mastermind was designed by a TV producer who as a prisoner of war had to answer three questions whenever he was interrogated: name, rank and number. These questions are how each of the contestants begin their first round. Each contestant gives name, occupation and specialist topic and this introduction establishes the interrogation style of the programme.

The first recording was at Liverpool University in 1972 and shown on BBC1. It was aired in a late night slot because it was thought too high-brow for a family audience. (If you do not know how schedulers break up the day go to Section 4.) When it was moved to prime time the audience numbers rose and so it stayed there. The original presenter was Magnus Magnussen. He came from Iceland but had lived in Scotland for many years and had a rather professorial persona often wearing a tweed suit with grey out of control hair.

The premise is five contestants compete against each other and the clock to answer as many questions correctly as possible. Each sits in turn in the famous chrome and black leather chair in a pool of light reminiscent of film noir interrogation scenes and is quizzed on their specialist subject (which they 'gen' up on) for 2 minutes and then in the second round they have two minutes on general knowledge questions. The other contestants sit in a row at the edge of the circle of light waiting their grilling. They are seen approaching the chair as the next contestant is announced. The shows are recorded in various celebrity venues such as university halls and so establish the gravitas of the programme through location as well as *mise-en-scène*. It also means that the set and crew have to be moved around the country rather than be in one place and this must add to the cost of the programme.

Like other quiz shows *Mastermind* has coined phrases that entered the general vernacular such as 'I've started so I'll finish', which the quizmaster says when he is half way through a question and the bell goes for the two minutes being up; and 'Pass' which a contestant says when they can't give an answer and don't want to waste time, as the key to success is to answer as many questions as possible in the two minutes. The passes are added up and counted against the contestant if there is a draw.

The questioning takes place like a film noir interrogation with the contestant and presenter in pools of light and the audience in darkness so using chiaroscuro lighting. The sound track is powerful with sonorous beats. It is called *Approaching Menace* (Neil Richardson). The most famous contestant of the original run was a London Cabbie called Fred Housego who won in 1980. Why do you think Fred became a famous winner?

The show's first run ended on terrestrial television in 2001 and moved to The Discovery Channel. This allowed viewers to play along with a new interactive feature. But it returned to BBC2 in 2003 with a new quizmaster John Humphreys, famous for his abrasive interviewing technique on Radio 4's flagship morning current

NOTES:

affairs programme *Today*. The format continues with 12 initial rounds, four quarter finals and the final. In 2004 a young person's version was introduced for contestants between 10 and 11. *Junior Mastermind* is also hosted by John Humphries.

So what does Mastermind tell us about society? This is what Len Masterman said about the original series:

> 'So, in Mastermind (BBC), for example, the single chair, the pool of light, the clipped impersonal tones of the questioner, the cutting to ever tighter close-ups of the contestants, all contribute to dominant and oppressive associations of knowledge and learning with interrogation, humiliation and fear of failure. These associations are validated and legitimised by the formal university settings in which the show takes place, and by *their* connotative links with the importance of factual recall within the show, as well as with the frequently absurd specialisms, and predominantly middle-class backgrounds of the contestants (the odd cabbie or tube driver amongst them simply attesting to the opportunities for upward-mobility which approved knowledge can bring with it).' (Masterman, 1985, p.204).

Do you think Masterman approved of the quiz show or not?

Which words/phrases suggest approval or disapproval?

If you can, view a current *Mastermind*. Do you recognise the same elements in the programme that Masterman described or has it changed? Superficially within the format there appears to be little changed. However read what was written about it recently: 'Poor Magnus Magnusson [the long running presenter] must be turning in his grave …featured many intellectually challenging subjects. This week, a contestant chose Jennifer Aniston as her specialist subject….The BBC argues naturally, that it wants to broaden the appeal of the quiz….Turning the programme into an up-market pub quiz is all very well, but does it deserve to retain its grandiose title?' ('Mediocre-mind', Editorial Comment, *Daily Telegraph*, 15/08/07). It seems that this writer is suggesting that even *Mastermind* is being dumbed down in order to entertain more and inform less. Do you agree that answering questions on Jennifer Aniston is less worthy than answering questions on William Shakespeare?

This idea of what is knowledge and what is education is at the heart of some of the debates around quiz shows. Masterman claimed for example that *Mastermind*'s connotations of set, presenter, style, competitors and so on led to

ideological themes which reflected class, gender and racial representations and a de-humanised, hierarchical and oppressive construction of what counts as learning and intelligence. These ideas reflect and construct meanings, values and beliefs about the real world and education. This is a complex issue and is discussed more fully in Section 7 Debates.

6.4 *University Challenge* (BBC2 1962–87; 1994–present)

Even though it does not give away money, *University Challenge* is one of the most successful television quiz shows. The home audience runs into the low millions. It began in 1962 and the first series was won by Leicester University. The show was based on an American show called *College Bowl*. The first presenter until 1987 was Bamber Gascoigne, who had a soft academic style of presenting. The show then was mothballed until 1994 when it returned with Jeremy Paxton as presenter. Paxman has a particular brusque manner and will comment on the more inept answers when he feels they should be known. His phrase 'Come on. Come on – I need an answer now!' is regularly used. Jeremy Paxman shows his exasperation and comments on the types of knowledge used. I recently watched a *University Challenge* in which the music round was on popular music and Paxman said words to the effect of – let's get this over as quickly as possible – indicating his opinion of popular music.

It stands out as being quite old fashioned in its approach to the genre. There are no gimmicks, the questions are quite intellectual and there are no big prizes. In the past dictionaries, T-shirts and a stainless steel trophy have been in the offing. Out of the 200 teams that apply annually a test paper weeds them down to 36 from which 28 are chosen. The bottom scorers have a second chance to be selected to go on by the subjective decisions of the producers on how the team will perform in front of the camera. There are eight people who set the questions and who are mainly from academic backgrounds. Peter Guuyn the producer in 2002 said 'As a rule of thumb, we expect the students to have a crack at 60 to 70% of the questions so it is purposefully quite hard' (Gordon, 2002, p.11).

In spite of its format the show has had its exciting moments. One team answered only 'Trotsky' and 'Marx' as a protest against what they perceived as the show's elitism and their university was then banned for over 20 years. There have been some contestants who have become famous. One well known one was Stephen Fry. Others were Clive James, David Mellor, Malcolm Rifkind (the latter two became

Case Studies

politicians) and John Simpson the chief BBC Foreign Correspondent. The show though has attracted other controversy. In 1999 Lance Howard who had made a career out of entering quiz shows over 22 years joined the Open University as a student in order to become a team member. Why should people feel that this was unfair?

The format is the questioner sitting at a desk with piles of questions on cards. The two teams are seated to his right behind two long desks with their names in front of them. At the beginning a starter question 'for 10' marks is given and the first team to answer this correctly gets the chance to build up their score by answering a series of questions on a similar topic before the next starter question is asked. Contestants have to press a buzzer to answer the starter question and are not allowed to consult with their team mates; however, they can consult as a team for the other questions and the captain gives the answer. Like *The Weakest Link* a male voice over gives information, this time the name and university of the first person to press the buzzer to answer the starter question.

The elements are typical of a quiz show with lighting and colour, camera positions and a studio audience who are usually partisan supporting the teams.

Set in 1985 the film *Starter for Ten* (2006) centres on a working class student at Bristol University. The film is nominally about qualifying for the TV quiz show *University Challenge*, but it is also about class divisions in social, love and intellectual life represented by the quiz show so it is useful for looking at issues of representation (see Section 7).

6.5 *Who Wants to be a Millionaire?* (ITV 1998–present)

Celador, its makers, spent two years trying to get this show on air and it was finally taken up by ITV in 1998. Subsequently it has been called by the *New York Times* as 'England's most successful cultural export in the last 30 years' (Boddy, quoted in Creeber, 2002, p.81). It was an immediate hit partly through clever scheduling. The first ten shows went out on consecutive nights. By the end of 2000 it was in 35 countries and sold as a format in 45 more including the notoriously difficult American market. 'That a game show had appeared in a US prime schedule was extraordinary. That is came from Britain was simply incredible' (Balzagette, 2005, p.122). The producer Michael Davies had tried to re-launch *The $64,000 Question* in America but had been stumped because people were unwilling to risk all to double their prize money. When he saw *Millionaire* he realised that this solved the risk taking problem: "The multiple-choice answers and the various lifelines enabled anyone, however ill-educated, genuinely to take risks and try to go all the way' (Balzagette, 2005, p.123). Eventually the show was shown in the summer of 1999 by Disney-ABC and boosted ratings by 9%. It lifted ABC for the first time from third to first position in the network ratings. The industry estimated that ABC's annual profits from the show at between $400 million and $600 million, an amount greater than the typical annual profits of an entire US TV network (Creeber, 2002).

The show's Indian version was broadcast five times a week in 2000 and gained an 87% share of the audience. It was shown on Murdoch's Star Plus satellite channel in India and Star's profits from this one programme were more than the combined earnings for all the other Star TV channels in India.

Why do you think this show is so successful over so many different cultures?

NOTES:

In the early years in the UK contestants were selected after a telephone and studio qualifying quizzes. Those who were successful came onto the show to answer increasingly difficult questions. They were seated opposite the host (Chris Tarrant) in an amphitheatre design with high tech *mise-en-scène*. Mood music and smoke have been used to enhance the feeling of tension. Contestants double their prize money every time they get a correct answer. Contestants can get help three times by asking the audience, phoning a friend or eliminate two of the incorrect answers called 50:50. Top prize winners are few. The first quiz show millionaire was a London 'housewife' Judith Keppel who now appears in another quiz called *Eggheads*.

The format starts with easy questions so that everyone watching feels that they could also be a contestant, unlike the format of *Mastermind* where you have to have specialist knowledge. During the first three series more than 10,000,000 people called in keeping 4,800 lines busy. This allowed a profit of £1,250,000 (Sutcliffe, 1999). At its height it was drawing in 19 million viewers. As the contestants reach the £1,000 mark Tarrant begins to tease and put doubts into their minds and add to the tension. The next safety ledge is £32,000 and it is here the hook to the next programme would occur.

Millionaire brought in a high proportion of ABC1s (these are people who come from socio-economic classes who are higher earners) which ITV does not normally attract and who are not normally quiz viewers. (See Section 3 on audiences.)

Like the big winning American shows *Twenty Twenty* and *$64,000 Question* the large prizes attracted cheating. On 10 September 2001 a Major Charles Ingram won one million pounds. The recording was analysed by the producers of the show and it became apparent that possibly Ingram was being helped to choose the right answer by the coughing of fellow contestants. The prize was withdrawn and Ingram and his 'accomplices' were taken to court. Like others this show has branched out into a celebrity version.

6.6 *Countdown* (Channel 4 1982–to date)

Countdown is another long running show. It was the first show to be shown on Channel 4 when it began in November 1982. Here are some facts about it from its web site:

A contestant won 19 games on the trot. Its appeal spans the generations. An eight year old and an 87 year old have played. One of the producers had been a contestant. Countdown was honoured in 2004 with a House of Commons reception in recognition of its contribution to numeracy and literacy. In 2003 it was voted Channel 4's best show of all times in a *Radio Times* poll. *Countdown* is now hosted by Des O'Connor with Carol Vorderman who was a founding presenter with Richard Whitely. It celebrated its 25 years on Channel 4 in 2007.

Judith Keppel on *Millionaire* (far left); Carol and Des on *Countdown* (left)

This show has fairly low production values. It could almost be played in the local village hall. Quickness of mind is the key to success. There are two contestants pitted against each other with the quiz master giving questions which allow them to choose cards. Carol Vorderman, the assistant, has become a personality in her own right rather than just being the stereotypical glamorous assistant (at the time of going to press, Vorderman is considering her future with the show). She turns cards over as the contestants choose and then they have to make up words with the chosen letters. If a word is questionable it is checked in a dictionary by an observer and there is a celebrity guest who will also pose questions for the home audience to answer. The quiz master gives a hook question from one half of the show to the second part after the commercial break to keep people watching. Carol Vorderman uses her mathematical skills to check the formula that the contestants come up with in the numeracy question.

This very simple format has been a mainstay of the schedules and helps Channel 4 to attract an afternoon audience pre-prime time. Its popularity has recently been in decline particularly after the death of Richard Whitley, the long serving presenter. Des O'Connor his replacement is a well known presenter and personality who would seemingly appeal to the

Case Studies

target audience. Does the decline in popularity reveal that *Countdown* was popular because of its presenter rather than its format?

The shows discussed above usually have 'ordinary' people from the general public as contestants. However, some of the most popular shows are where the contestants are celebrities. Even these have alternative appeal. Channel 4 chief Stuart Cosgrove said: 'There is a big difference between a knowledge-based quiz such as *A Question of Sport* and a show such as *Have I Got News For You* which is more about comedy than correct answers' (quoted in Morgan and Weale, 1999, p.14).

6.7 *They Think It's All Over* (it is now) (BBC1 1995–2006)

This was a celebrity sports quiz produced by a company called Talkback Productions. The title comes from a famous comment made by the television commentator Kenneth Wolstenholme during the 1966 Soccer World Cup final when the crowd began to come onto the pitch before the referee had called time. The show was built upon the clever responses and comedy generated by the two teams. However, although this appeared spontaneous the producers of the programme for BBC have acknowledged that help was given 'off screen'. Both the team captains and guests were given off-camera help and the presenter's comments were usually scripted. The panellists also got a preview of video clips used in some of the rounds up to three hours before the show. The producers said that the show was for entertainment and as many of the guests were usually personalities unused to television studios or this format they would simply not be able to 'perform' without this help.

Other similar shows have admitted that what the viewers sees is not a reflection of reality. *Dictionary Corner* and *A Game of Two Halves* (Scotland) have admitted that the contestants get a preview of some of the questions so that they can prepare entertaining answers. This is defined

as 'giving viewers value for money' (T. Cowan, team captain of *A Game of Two Halves*). The preparation is even more rehearsed in *Never Mind the Buzzcocks* (BBC2). The guests are briefed before it is filmed and the contestants have two dummy runs before going on air. The anchor person has to give the impression of giving off the cuff remarks but is in fact reading off autocue. Much of the spontaneous material is cut because it is too laden with expletives. The so-called 'zoo television' is in fact planned chaos.

A Question of Sport has sports personalities in two teams and is hosted by Sue Barker, herself a very good tennis player in her youth. Unlike other celebrity shows this quiz records without any preparation of the contestants. The takeouts where the contestants have muffed answers or perhaps have been given over to giggles are often used for a separate programme.

6.8 *Have I Got News For You* (BBC2 1990–present)

Produced by an independent company Hat Trick Productions for BBC *Have I Got News For You* had at one time 12 million viewers watching. Following Angus Deayton's publicity problems the quiz is now chaired by different personalities from both entertainment and politics. It has as its team captains Ian Hislop (editor of *Private Eye*, a political satirical magazine) and Paul Merton, a comedian. Guest team members are pulled from the entertainment and political world. They are often the butt of jokes and comments from the chairperson and have to hold their own in somewhat gladitorial banter. Paula Yates famously called Hislop 'spawn of the devil'. The comments can be quite near the bone and lawyers are always present (from both the BBC and Hat Trick Productions) to check the content. Hislop has been before the courts accused of libel for articles written in *Private Eye*. If something is said that is potentially difficult Hislop is sometimes recorded saying 'But as we all know, that suggestion is totally untrue'. There is a mix of serious comment and surreal humour with the added

NOTES:

spice of a frisson of potentially libellous comment which has made this celebrity quiz show popular.

The two teams sit on either side of the presenter backed by a montage of distorted news photographs and headlines. They have rounds of questions on topical issues in the news. However, it is not the correct answers which are the focus of the show but the quick wit of the team 'captains', the satire and the way that the other celebrities cope with their pungent remarks. The presenter has a prepared comedic script which they read off auto-cue, but the remarks of Merton and Hislop often appear to be off the cuff and they frequently look to the studio audience for responses. The two captains are an interesting pairing. They represent different classes. Merton is more working class in style and Hislop is more middle class/public school boy. They both use the presenter as a butt to their jokes and their different class style. Like other celebrity quizzes HIGNY has been accused of being slightly laddish in its humour.

6.9 *QI* (BBC2 2003–present)

This is an even more surreal quiz show than *HIGNFY*. This quiz show has celebrity comics who answer general knowledge questions. They sit in two teams of three either side of the question master. The chair is Stephen Fry who imposes his particular personality on the show. He behaves rather like a fatherly university don dealing with some recalcitrant students.

The title connotes the phrase IQ (intelligence quotient), which was a way of assessing people's intelligence but actually stand for 'Quite Interesting'. Fry sits between the two teams and asks questions but his scoring is particularly random. The point seems to be to have clever and interesting conversation rather than to win a game. This quiz show could be called a **post-modern** style of show as it has an eclectic range of knowledge and randomness in scoring.

6.10 More Recent Shows – *The Great Pretender* (ITV1 2007)

There are many other quizzes which come and go such as *School's Out* (BBC1) a celebrity charity quiz, as well as late night ITV phone-ins which appear under the heading of ITV Play after midnight. New programmes are tried out regularly. *The Great Pretender* (ITV) began in November 2007. The name has links with a song and also suggests that the game will in some way be about deception. Hosted by Chris Tarrant of *Millionaire* fame, it had no audience and lasted one hour. It began by being shown in the 5–6 p.m. prime time early evening slot, just before the news, on sequential nights. This programme had echoes of *The Weakest Link* in its format and maybe ITV's attempt to capture audiences away from the BBC. The six contestants answer general knowledge questions and their right answers add money to the pot. They have to keep judging who is winning as they are not told if the answers given are right or wrong. During the early rounds two contestants are voted off. The person who has the highest score has to pretend that they are not the highest scorer so that the others guess wrongly who is and then the leader takes the money. If the others guess right about who has the highest score they get the money and the pretender gets nothing. The quiz therefore relied partly on good memory and partly on deception. It also depended upon the ability of ordinary people to keep a discussion/argument going. You do not need to be the most knowledgeable to stay in *The Great Pretender*, which like other shows is a hybrid of game and quiz show.

The set is blue and futuristic. Tarrant sits in a large white swivel chair facing the semi-circle of contestants. Unlike Robinson he is genial and jocular, but he does interview the contestants and they do have to defend and justify their decisions quite determinedly. Behind the set there is a chat room for the contestants to argue over who they think got the most answers right. Between rounds a male voice over announces the score and the total money won so far. The value of the prize money is in the low thousands so like *Weakest Link* it is not life changing.

Case Studies

6.11 *Duel* (ITV1 2008)

New formats are being looked for continuously. In 2008 the latest one on ITV was *Duel*:

'Duel, based on a French format, will see contestants battle head to head in a bid to win a "big money jackpot". The broadcaster said the quiz would create the "ultimate test of self confidence and nerve as players face total elimination from the show if they make just one error of judgement". …Even though Ant and Dec's company will produce the series, an ITV spokeswoman said they would not be fronting it "at the moment."… "At the moment it is not an Ant and Dec vehicle," she said. "Their company is moving to produce more shows that aren't fronted by them….No presenter is lined up at the moment." …ITV's controller of entertainment Duncan Gray has commissioned eight one-hour episodes of the quiz that are set to air early next year. The broadcaster has long wanted to find another major quiz show to sit alongside the revamped *Who Wants to be a Millionaire?*, which it has just signed to a new two-year deal. "We are always on the look out for good quiz shows and this is one," said the spokeswoman. The quiz format, created by French production company French TV, which is represented by the William Morris agency, has received a lot of interest internationally, with a major US network also set to announce it has commissioned it in the next few days. …"It's a compelling game which I hope will make a great TV show. I'm delighted that both French TV and Gallowgate Productions will chose to work with ITV to put Duel on air in the UK." …Gallowgate produces most of Ant and Dec's shows, including quiz PokerFace and All Star Cup.' (Holmwood, *Media Guardian*, 7 September 2007)

Duel began in January 2008 with its final show in the series on Saturday 5 April 2008. It was scheduled from 8 p.m. to 9 p.m. and hosted by Nick Hancock who was already well known as a quiz host; 8 p.m. puts it in prime time but later than *The Weakest Link* or *Eggheads*, for example.

Saturday night also puts it into a particular slot. If you can watch this show (at the time of going to press, ITV have not recommissioned it) you might speculate on why this scheduling was chosen. This is one comment: 'It is a neat mechanic (covering multiple choice answers with chips) which you COULD turn into a nice, simple daytime quiz show, but it has nothing else to suggest it is a Saturday night show' (www.digitalspy.co.uk/forums).

The title sequence shows a silhouette of two people standing back to back as if about to have a duel. Each duel consists of two contestants face to face in the classic gladiatorial positioning. They have twenty brightly coloured poker chips each. The contestants answer multiple choice questions simultaneously. The questions are shown on screen so that the audience at home can play along as well. The contestants cannot see the other's answers, because of a barrier between them, unlike the audience who can see what answers both contestants are betting on. The barrier is lowered once they have both 'locked down'. The placing of chips is shown on screen by graphics but also we occasionally have a 'god-shot' to look down on the playing table.

In choosing the right answer there is a slow build up with contestants hovering over possible answers to play their chips. Once they have 'locked down' they cannot change their mind. There is a sense of double bluff as with poker in that someone might know the answer but will appear to hesitate in the hope that this will force their opponent to play more chips and so lose these chips for future games. If one presses the 'accelerator' the other has to decide quickly where to place their chips.

If a contestant gets a question wrong they are eliminated. If they are both right they carry on playing. The winner of the duel decides whether to cash in their chips or to try to add to their winnings by facing a new contestant. Hancock as the questioner is positioned in between the two contestants. All three are standing. Hancock asks the questions but also engages in conversation

NOTES:

with the contestants to find out about them; he walks around a little creating more dynamism visually. These conversations create personalities so as the audience at home you can side with one of the duellists. The contestants will also talk to each other to encourage the idea of bluffing.

The lighting around the audience is low key and we only see the backs of the audience as the camera swings around behind them – this positions the studio audience as us sitting at home. The table is spot lit. Fluorescent pinks, blues, greens appear around the table helping to create an exciting visual look in something which is fundamentally quite static. Behind Hancock are graphic stars shining and glinting in a dark background and at relevant times ethereal female voices are heard and a beat like a ticking clock, increasing the tension through the non-diegetic sounds.

In the final in 2008 the jackpot of £166,000 was won after the fourth duel and fireworks were set off around the duel 'arena' to celebrate.

To find out more about this show if it is not currently playing go to: www.itv.com/ITVPlay/Gameshows/Duel/.

6.12 Conclusion

These case studies cover a range of different styles and target audiences, but they are not exhaustive. You are probably aware of other examples. If you are more familiar with another show do some research on it and analyse how it works for the audience. Remember to consider the channel and scheduling as well as the micro elements such as the style of questions and the presenter. Use a check list like the ones listed in the genre and textual analysis section for ideas.

References

Balzagette, P. (2005) *Billion Dollar Game: How Three Men Risked it All and Changed the Face of Television*, London: Time/Warner Books.

Gordon, B. 'Universally challenged: Forty Years on, the Unashamedly Highbrow Quiz is More Popular than Ever, says Bryony Gordon', *Daily Telegraph*, 23 March 2002, InfoTrac, Thomson Gale.

Holmwood, L., 'Duel', *Media Guardian*, 7 September 2007.

Knight, K. 'The Meanest Quiz Show', *Sunday Express*, 4 March 2001.

Morgan, K. and Weale, N. 'A Game of Two Half-Truths; forget the quick-fire answers…most TV comedy quiz shows rehearse answers with guests. *Daily Record*, Glasgow, 22nd February

1999 InfoTrac, Thomson Gale.

Stafford, R. 'Breaking down *The Weakest Link?*', *In the Picture*, No. 40, pp.19-20.

Sutcliffe, T. 'Who Wants to be a Millionaire? (The Bloke on the Left Talking to Chris Tarrant Does – and So Do 19 Million Others)', *The Independent*, 2 September 1999.

Viner, B. 'Three Wise Men. A Star and a Miracle; the Extraordinary Birth of *Who Wants To Be a Millionaire?* the Quiz Show Worshipped by a Nation', *The Independent*, 23 December 1999 InfoTrac, Thomson Gale.

www.bbc.co.uk/entertainment/mastermind/history

Student Activities

Activity 6a: Discussion

What type of person would want to appear on *The Weakest Link*?

Consider age, gender, class, ethnicity, etc. What type of person would not want to go on the show? Discuss the pros and cons of being a quiz contestant.

Activity 6b: Persona

Watch three extracts from _The Weakest Link_ – the opening and closing sequences plus one other, such as Anne Robinson's interview with a contestant.

In the first column below write words and phrases to describe the **persona** of the presenter.

Re-watch the same sequences and in the second column note the **technical details and language** that help to construct this persona.

Persona	Technical Codes

Using this primary research write a paragraph to answer the question:

'How is the persona of the presenter created in _The Weakest Link?_'

Support your points with detailed evidence from the extracts you have studied.

This exercise can be done with other quiz presenters and then the different personas can be compared to illustrate how they influence the style and tone of their respective quizzes.

(Teacher's note: If the students are finding this difficult you can give the basic structure omitting the italicised words and ask them to fill in suitable words in the gaps. For less able students a list of possible missing words can be given to fill in the gaps,

e.g. Anne Robinson has a _fierce and rather scary persona_. This is created by the use of _low angle_ shots which create a feeling of _power_. She uses an _accusatory_ mode of address such as 'are you really lucky?' Her dress code is _dark, long flowing robes_ which connote a _witch-like_ character, etc.)

Representation and Debates

Introduction

This section looks at some of the complex debates that circulate around the media and links them to the television quiz show genre. It particularly focuses on issues of representation.

In society our position, how we view others, the way we approach issues such as representation and media effects is dependent upon our gender, age, class, ethnicity as well as contextual factors like education. These positions are constructed through **discourses**. This means the languages (linguistic, technical, genre, etc.) used in the media that help construct meanings and that combine and circulate around social interaction. But languages are not neutral. They are shared systems that can signify relationships and representations. They are bound up with the idea of power which can support or challenge dominant beliefs (ideologies) about such things as family values, the worth of competition and what winning signifies. With the mass media the power is in the repetition of the message and its universality. **Realism** is a key issue here. Nothing we see in the media is 'real'; it is a re-presentation of a reality through selection and construction. Often we forget this when we are using the media. For example, a quiz show has to fit a time-slot, audiences warmed-up, contestants selected – everything is constructed.

Remember though that these are not monolithic one way systems as you will have discovered by studying audiences. Active audiences use the media to gratify needs. There are negotiated and oppositional readings that can be used by audiences to make sense of the world, both mediated and real. We therefore have to be careful not to rely on simplistic readings of texts.

7.1 Context

Television programmes reflect the context in which they appear. Like other television genres, such as police dramas or soap operas the quiz show **articulates** in different ways with society.

For example, they articulate with the following:

- Education – our understanding of what it means to be educated.

- Consumerism – there is a promise of reward but without the wait.

- Social relationships and class – we can achieve whatever our circumstances, even a taxi driver can become 'mastermind'.

- Status – there is the promise of celebrity status without the work or the talent necessary to become a star.

Therefore a quiz show interacts with social discourses, beliefs and power as well as reflects the particular needs and structures of society.

This perhaps can be more clearly seen by looking at early quizzes. The 1950s quiz shows were very popular on US television at a time in which the numbers of televisions were expanding rapidly giving popular access to the medium. It was also the same time that a Cold War was being fought between Communism and Capitalism based upon technology and science, with nuclear capability and the atom bomb being pivotal to this 'war'. Knowledge based upon science and technology was seen to be the key to victory and the quiz show represented the idea of knowledge in a popular form. And just like the heroes of the Soviet Revolution in Sergei Eisenstein's 1920s films had to look heroic as representatives of the proletariat, so the heroes of the American TV quiz shows had to represent the clean-cut all American intellectual hero. In addition contestants were able to win big, life-changing, prizes so their individual intellectual 'work' was seen to bring financial success important in a capitalist system. This approach to quiz shows indicates how the genre could be said to reflect society and articulate with the needs and the beliefs of the audiences.

7.2 High and Low Culture

One of the most important debates in the mass media rests upon beliefs about the social values of different types of cultural activity and this is intertwined with issues of power. The difference in status is significant in understanding the values we as a society place on certain types of knowledge. John Birt, once Director-General of the BBC, speaking at the Edinburgh International Television Festival in 2005 was reported to have said that 'British television has become increasingly cynical and cruel and has abandoned the intellectual high ground' and 'in an apparent swipe at BBC's *Test the Nation*, hosted by Anne Robinson, he said: "Yes. It is fun occasionally to have competitions for viewers or listeners to vote on the best this or the best that. But please, let us not tabloidise our intellectual life"' (Born, 'TV's Crude Culture of Cruelty, by Birt' *Daily Mail*, 27 August 2005).

This statement indicates how quiz shows can be seen as representative of society and are used as a way of labelling and making value judgements about contemporary mores. So for Birt a certain type of 'tabloid' quiz show stands for dumbing down of popular culture. This is not a new phenomenon. In discussing the early television quiz show Sue Holmes states: 'With their often large cash prizes and the incorporation of "gambling", the genre was attacked by critics for fostering a morally unhealthy attitude toward money, rewarding trivial displays of knowledge, and engaging participants in exploitative and "degrading' performances"' (Holmes, 2005 from www.birth-of-tv.org/birth/).

7.3 Fate and Luck – How to Move Mountains; or Make it Quick

In the past the 'folk' heroes of popular quiz shows were ones apparently from the working classes or less wealthy and therefore without the advantages of the cultural capital given by a good education. In the intellectual quizzes the majority of winners were generally of middle class origin or university educated. The folk heroes therefore won in spite of every disadvantage, like the taxi driver who became Mastermind. In *Quiz Show* (1994, Redford) as we enter the film the current 'champion' has become a folk hero. He is a Jewish ex G.I. without a college education. We see him walking down the street in Queens being greeted by his neighbours and cheered for his success in the show.

Is this still true today? Are the winners of quizzes folk heroes in the same way or is there a different attitude to quiz heroes?

It is not only work, education or endeavour that brings success. Lady Luck does have a say, whether the right questions come up, for example. Sometimes luck can over-ride the knowledge element of the quiz game, particularly where the quiz slides into a game. 'Luck' is also not without ideological meaning because it hides the inequalities inherent in the structures of the quiz game. We might think that one person won because they got the 'lucky break' or 'Lady Luck' was with them, not because they had a better education or a more privileged upbringing. Fiske (1987, p.270) suggests that 'The hegemonic function of luck is not just to minimize the personal sense of failure, but, more importantly, to demonstrate that the rewards of the system are, in fact, available to all, regardless of talent, class, gender, race, and so on.' This means that the function of luck is to hide inequalities.

Most of us have 'tried our luck', have gambled at some time be, it a raffle ticket or a lottery number. Gambling is about achieving without working, relying on luck and can of course be addictive. This is why the British regulators have had concerns with phone-in quizzes which they see as games of chance rather than quizzes.

Even in the 1960s the Pilkington Report, still steeped in the ideologies of John Reith and Public Service Broadcasting, was critical of ITV for its reliance on quiz shows that endorsed a culture of greed and consumption which relied on the idea of taking a chance rather than on pure knowledge. By the 1970s and 80s the Thatcherite ideals had begun to lead to the end, or at least the beginning of the end, of the Reithian philosophy of the three pillars of education, information as well as entertainment in public service broadcasting and the dominance of consumption and demand.

The current commercialisation, driven by convergence and digital technology, of television has continued the weakening of the PSB ethos and with it the perception that even the BBC, which historically set the standard of high cultural values in broadcasting, has had to succumb to commercial pressures. To illustrate this we can see the media comment when a contestant chose Jennifer Aniston as her specialist topic on *Mastermind*: 'what was once thought to be the most rigorous quiz on British television …the programme's producer, defended the show saying it had always had a "balance of high brow and populist subjects"' (Martin, *The Daily Telegraph*, 5 August 2007).

This comment illustrates that even a minor genre such as quiz shows is seen as a barometer of the values we place on and the distinction between high and low culture.

Representation and Debates

7.4 Stereotyping

One area of beliefs (ideologies) which is much debated in the media is that of representation and **stereotyping**. Today we are very familiar with issues such as race and gender stereotypes. But being aware does not mean they have disappeared. What happens is that they re-appear in new manifestations. Stereotyping can work by presenting us with fixed and simple signifiers that become associated with a whole group. A stereotype distorts by simplification and by exaggeration areas such as physical appearance, behaviour and actions and links them with key social identities such as race and gender. It is then repeated through many other texts. So we can have the class 'geek' who is often given glasses and unfashionable clothes to wear in media texts like cartoons and soaps. You can probably collect quite a few other stereotypes.

The issue of representation can be seen in quiz shows. For example in the past, hosts of quiz shows were usually male and participants were often white, male and middle class and this was seen to deliver messages about authority, education, knowledge, society and gender roles to audiences. Do you believe this is still so?

See Activity 7a: Primary Quantitative Research

Although who and what we read give us messages it is who is choosing these representations and who is behind the camera in terms of producers and programme-makers, which is just as important a question to ask. Are a particular group more likely to appear because they are being chosen (albeit unconsciously) by someone who picks out particular groups or faces or hair or…doesn't like red! If other faces, etc., are not seen and are absent from our screens do they become invisible to us? The corollary of the research in 7a is which groups are not represented; which are absent or invisible? What does this say about them? Are these groups not intellectually able to participate in quiz shows, for example? Or are there other reasons such as culture?

If you have access to the BBC *Race in the Frame* publication there is a good example of a game show called *Blind Date* that shows the effect that such stereotypes have on us. Cilla Black was the host and contestants put themselves forward to have a blind date with one of three contestants that they chose just by their voice and answers to questions. On one occasion a young man who was obviously very middle class – he even wore a bow tie and blazer – picked a young black girl. The audience's reaction was 'breathtaking'! What would have been your reaction if you had been the contestant and picked a Chinese, Black, White, Indian, Arab, Gypsy…? How many of these ethnic groups do you frequently see on quiz and game shows? In the same pack Greg Philo (Glasgow Media Group) and representatives from the BBC talk about the limited participant types in game shows and show how choices made influence the types of contestant and therefore who we believe should be on the shows.

My students looked at this issue and felt that a programme like *The Weakest Link* had quite a range of different groups represented. This perhaps reveals how the BBC as a PSB has tried to engage with these issues and be more inclusive. Is this true of other quizzes on other channels?

Representation is a key issue and Richard Dyer (1985) asked the questions who is being represented by whom, to whom and for whom. This is a good summary but quite an abstract list of questions. It might be useful to subdivide these into the following:

- Who is in control of the representation – that is the producers and owners of the text in which they appear?

- What codes and conventions are being used, such as the technical languages of lighting and dress codes?

- Who is being represented in terms of who they represent as a group – such as gender, class, ideas, institution?

NOTES:

- Who is reading this representation; that is, who is looking at those being represented? What audiences are there for these texts?

- How is the reader positioned to read the text? Are they being asked to support or condemn, applaud or denigrate?

- Are there other similar representations as in other shows from the same genre? How often do we see/not see particular types?

(adapted from Helsby, 2005)

Trying to answer these questions requires an analytical approach and one where you stand back from your own beliefs and prejudices. This is quite difficult. Ideology happens behind our backs.

Very often there are groups from which we feel alienated for reasons of class, colour, region and so on, but often if we meet these people we realise that we have had misconceptions about them. Where do we get these ideas? Obviously the media is one very powerful conveyer of messages, although our own peers and family are also influential. Most Media Studies takes a constructionist approach to representation and analyses the texts semiotically as well as looking at the context and the discursive formations which are constructed around these texts.

So representation is about construction, distortion and repetition of ideas and beliefs. This is not only about representation of different people but also of institutions and ideas such as education, knowledge and culture.

See Activity 7b: *Starter for Ten*

7.5 Gendered and Cultural Specific Knowledge

Quiz shows with their focus and emphasis on knowledge and information have often been associated with gendering of knowledge. Critics of the genre suggest that the definition of knowledge as 'facts' does not allow for explanation or reflection which might be more associated with a female trait or with a particular culture. The nature of awarding points and having clear cut answers means you cannot have a debate; the answer is obviously either right or wrong in order to award points. In addition critics have noted that the knowledge often reflects the 'social, cultural and national contexts' (Holmes, 2006, p.64) and perhaps does not reward other types of knowledge. So, in a multicultural society, can we have a 'fair' quiz?

It is suggested therefore that the reason that quiz culture is perceived as largely a male domain is

because of the type of questions and testing. The gender imbalance is a concern for broadcasters who are clearly bound to try to have equal access. Dawn Ellis, a Radio 4 quiz producer said, 'It's a real problem at the BBC….We have people sitting around saying, "Why aren't there more women?" and you do everything you can to persuade women to come on, but you still get far more men. On *Counterpoint* [a musical quiz on Radio 4] I've really struggled to get any women at all. There's no way you can do anything to make the quizzes female-friendly, like trying to think of questions that only women would know. That would be just insulting. You can't positively discriminate.' Richard Edis, producer of *Brain of Britain* on Radio 4, said 'We need 48 contestants a series and our best ever ratio was one woman to four men. Our worst was one to 12' (Thynne, 2006, p.19). Thynne suggests that it may be the perception of the contestants that is off-putting with the idea of the 'nerd' as the typical type, as in the film *Starter for Ten*. The 'nerd' is the quiz buff who can recite the top ten records in the past three decades. Edis stated that the archetypal contestant tended to be 'male, white, 45–55 librarian, civil servant or local government officer' (ibid.).

Are women better team players? Could the female instinct for conciliation rather than confrontation be a drawback in the quiz arena? Is it the competitive nature of the quiz that favours men or is there something more intangible such as the type of questions?

See Activity 7c: Gendered Questions

7.6 Class

'The focus on the relationship between knowledge, class and education and, by extension, … ideological implications…' (Fiske, 1987, p.266). Following World War 2 the education system had been part of re-building Britain and had been partly based upon the grammar school providing the opportunity for the bright but financially disadvantaged children to become equal with those who could afford private education. Similarly the quiz show allowed bright individuals who may have been disadvantaged culturally to have the opportunity to achieve status and economic benefit, i.e. prizes (ibid.).

But even though this myth existed the winners of quizzes like *Brain of Britain* mostly came from the 'well-educated'. The questions were usually based upon the classics, history, literature, science rather than on popular culture. *Millionaire*'s first three winners were certainly not local taxi driver or pub quiz types. Judith Keppel was the first person to reach the jackpot, 'critics in the quality press grumbled about the privileged nature of her background…conspires still to make private

Representation and Debates

education better than a state one....' (Holmes, 2006, p.66).

This is a difficult one, because access to education is nominally equal but of course there are always going to be differences in quality. Having watched several quiz shows do you believe the type of question in certain quizzes is weighted to private education rather than state education? Or are they weighted in terms of gender? (If you did Activity 2C look at your answers and discuss them in relation to ideas of representation.)

7.7 Dumbing Down

In contrast to the elitist criticism another strand in the on-going debate around media is that of the lowering of standards in our cultural life. The quiz shows were seen as having a '"deleterious effect on public taste" (*Evening Standard*, 26 May 1965) and an "affront to human dignity and intelligence" (*Daily Mail*, 1964)' (quoted in Holmes, 2006, p.55). These comments reveal the belief that commercial imperatives were perceived to have dumbed down popular taste through television. ITV had started in 1955 just ten years before and the link between Americanisation and the perception of dumbing down became more explicit as commercial television flourished. Waldeman, one time Head of Light Entertainment, said '"there would be no big American stuff here...."' (quoted in Holmes, 2006, p.59).

Even within the BBC there is a belief that 'standards' have dropped. In commenting about a Mastermind contestant choosing Jennifer Aniston as a specialist topic *The Daily Telegraph* correspondent stated, 'The explosion of populist subjects in the revived version of the BBC quiz show prompted accusations last night that the programme has been dumbed down' (Martin, *Daily Telegraph*, 15 August 2007). The March 2008 final had similar populist specialist topics.

These comments reveal the discourses of class, education and knowledge that circulate around quiz shows and show how meanings and beliefs about society are both generated and reinforced. Do you feel that contemporary quiz shows have lowered standards? What do you feel about a specialist topic being a celebrity? Does this just reflect changes in society rather than a qualitative difference in society? The debate is centred upon the opposition between education and entertainment. The quiz shows are based around the discourse of education but of course they are also shows that rely on entertainment to attract large audiences. The emphasis has moved from the education to the entertainment particularly by emphasising personalities. In America there has been a similar trend: '"They don't want the cool, composed type or the intelligent, well-informed citizen. They want the boobs"' (quoted in Mittell, 2004).

7.8 Types of Knowledge

So quiz shows use knowledge to separate winners and losers, but the types of knowledge are ideologically significant. Some ask for academic knowledge something only given with the cultural capital (Bourdieu) of a 'good' education. Other knowledge is factual, such as dates, names of mountains and so on and links to a particular view of being knowledgeable, that is, the retention of facts. This is less to do with education but still has the kudos attached of being able to recall facts under stress, as in an examination, which is what *Mastermind* does. These types of knowledge are quite narrow. However, there are other types of knowledge; that of the everyday such as is linked into popular culture and current events; and the knowledge that is gained through social interaction and work. We all know people who are 'uneducated' but who are experts in their field although their knowledge may not be accredited by certificates. This reveals hierarchies of knowledges.

NOTES:

Fiske (1987) suggested a hierarchy of quiz shows.

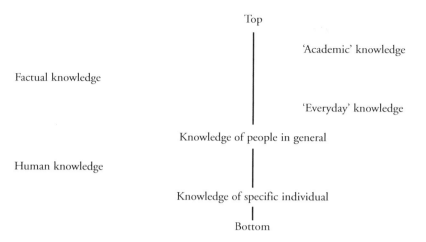

(Adapted from Fig 14.1, Fiske, 1987: 269)

The shows in the upper levels tend to be on prime time television whilst those lower down are shows which appear in the day time slots. 'As the "knowledge" becomes more democratized, so the popularity of the programmes shifts towards those with less social power' (Fiske, 1987, p.269). With these hierarchies of knowledge 'whether show-casing the knowledge of "experts" or inviting "ordinary" people to perform, the programmes incorporate a wide variety of cultural referents, which range from the gentility of the middle-class parlour game, the discourses of schooling and education, to the pleasures of fun, leisure and carnival' (Holmes, 2006, p.57).

ITV's populist approach and its more working class appeal led to criticism of the types of question asked; such as, 'which animals inhabit a hutch not a sty' (*The Times*, 1958, quoted in Holmes, 2006, p.68). A show like *Double Your Money* revealed a broadening of the range of participants both socially and in terms of gender. Subjects included the traditional academic ones but also railways, fashion, the Music Hall; in other words, knowledge that came from 'common social experience…rather than the education system' (Fiske, 1987, p.267). In fact *Double Your Money* (1955–68) rather undermined education by stating that 'it's so easy – even schoolchildren can play' (ibid.). Today if these hierarchies still exist are they still so clearly delineated?

A similar belief about the quiz show and its relationship to education was evident on American television. The promotional material highlighted the positive effects of a show like *Quiz Kids* on children's attitude to schooling. The shows were linked with 'positive social values and education' (Mittell, 2004, p.37). This was based upon the belief that these shows were 'spontaneous, ad-libbed, and featured

unrehearsed, fair competition' (ibid.) although it was proved that the children taking part were often rehearsed in their answers. In fact there was a seemingly tacit agreement between audiences and producers that as long as the rehearsing was not too evident audiences seemed to accept that coaching of contestants was inevitable to provide entertainment, such as with the light-hearted banter between presenter and contestant.

7.9 How Big? Regulating Prizes

The BBC has been continually concerned about the cost and underlying meanings attached to prizes. Holmes quotes Cecil McGivern, a Controller of Television, in response to *The Charlie Chester Show*'s (1950s) introduction of 'visual' prizes as saying: '"The prizes must in the greater majority be visual and of the type given at fairs (the better type of fairs, in accordance with BBC standards), e.g. large teddy bears but *not* an expensively dressed doll from Liberty's"' (Holmes, 2006, p.59).

This indicates the type of contestant that McGivern believed would take part in such shows in terms of class. The tabloid press referred to the 'idiot contestants and giveaway shows' (*The Daily Mail*, 1964, quoted in Holmes, 2006, p.68). The knowledge quiz shows therefore had an ambivalent reception amongst the voices of concern, what could be called the **hegemonic** lieutenants in charge of cultural values. The tension between the discourses around elitism and egalitarianism in education clearly reflected the social issues of the period. There was the belief that prizes in such shows as *Double Your Money* could help '"erase…the social differences implicit in the class-based, elite cultural knowledge of quiz shows"' (Hoerschelmann, 2000, quoted in Holmes, 2006, p.69).

Representation and Debates

These debates around quiz shows of the 1950s/60s may well have echoes with those around reality shows today. The use of ordinary people, the chance to be famous in Andy Warhol's phrase 'for fifteen minutes', the exploitative nature of the shows where contestants are manipulated and maybe humiliated, the opportunity to win something, the use of participant shows to attract audiences. All are present in reality shows as they were in quiz shows and have attracted similar criticisms.

This is not only about the media but reflects issues in society. For example, one of the criticisms of the last few years of sport in schools is that competitive games have been phased out in favour of individual achievement goals. For some this means that the team ethos has been dropped in favour of the first past the post, by fair means or foul, perhaps represented in the type of reality and quiz/game shows that we see on television.

7.10 Celebrities

Connected with this push towards individualism is that of the rise of the celebrity. One of the key debates in the study of media today is about the celebritisation of society. This idea is different from stardom. Could you suggest how?

The types (genres) and styles of programme on television have changed quite a lot over the last half century. In the past personalities did appear but they tended to be people who had a particular talent or expertise. Today we have people who are famous for being famous.

See Activity 7d: 1950s TV

If you have looked at some old presenters make a comparison with today's presenters. What do you notice that they have in common and what is different? Not just fashion and funny hairstyles! It is often easier to see ideologies at work when we are distanced from them. You will probably note ages, accents, language as well as attitude.

Celebrity is about using the media to feed stories and comment into a discourse that circulates within the media so building up an awareness of a personality who is famous for being famous. The personality may have some talent but talent is not the main criteria for their fame. Important people like politicians may well use celebrity style publicity to help their campaigns. What does this celebrity culture say about society? Are we more interested in fame than facts? There are lots of difficult questions here and ones which have no clear cut answers. It is worth keeping these ideas in mind whilst studying what is a seemingly innocuous, just for fun, programme to see if you can tease out some of the deeper issues that are involved.

7.11 Conclusion

As we have seen previously in Sections 4 and 5 television is the result of a range of choices and influences. Some of these are regulations, ownership and control, working practices, technology, cultural changes and aesthetics. As a result of these pressures and influences the mediation of the message influences the meanings of the message. A famous aphorism is 'the medium is the message' which Marshall McLuhan coined (*Understanding Media*, 1964). This means that the nature of the medium does not represent reality but a construction of signs which signify meanings. The type of medium through which the message is conveyed will influence the message. The media re-present life to us. The question to answer is how does the quiz show re-present society?

This discussion has raised issues about values, beliefs and knowledge. It has looked at the beliefs or ideologies about representation of class, gender and race, about the values associated with high and low culture, the meaning of education and the way it has ideological significance, about dumbing down and the celebritisation of what Habermas (1996) called 'the public sphere'. Quiz shows are not just cheap filler programmes, for Media Studies they provide an interesting

NOTES:

window into the power of the media and the way they reveal the values and beliefs of a society.

See Activity 7e: Spot the Message

References

Born, M. 'TV's Crude Culture of Cruelty, by Birt', *Daily Mail*, 27 August 2005.

Fiske, J. (1987) *Television Culture*, London: Methuen/Routledge.

Foucault, M. (1980) *Power/Knowledge*, Brighton: Harvester.

Martin, N. '*Mastermind* and a question of standards,' *Daily Telegraph*, 5 August 2007.

Mittell, J. (2004) *Genre and Television: From Cops to Cartoons in American Culture*, London: Routledge.

Habermas, J. (1996) 'The Public Sphere', in Marris, P. and Thornham, S. (eds) *Media Studies: A Reader*, Edinburgh: Edinburgh University Press.

Helsby, W. (ed.) (2005) *Understanding Representation*, London: BFI.

Thynne, J. (1996) 'Quizzes: Who's Answering? (Observations)', *New Statesman* (1), 18 December 2006: 19, InfoTrac OneFile, Thomson Gale.

Student Activities

Activity 7a: Primary Quantitative Research

Over a range of quiz shows count the number of different groups represented as presenters and contestants, such as men/women/white/black/Chinese/Asian/disabled/old/middle-aged/young etc. who are involved either as presenters or contestants. Which group(s) is dominant? What conclusions can you draw from this research?

Name of Quiz Show	Men or Women?	White or other ethnic origin	Old, young or middle-aged?	Which group(s) is dominant

Activity 7b: *Starter for Ten*

You might like to watch *Starter for Ten* (2006, Vaughan) at this point (see *University Challenge*, Section 6.3) and discuss the issues raised by the film in terms of representation of groups, particularly class.

Activity 7c: Gendered Questions

Can you draw up five questions which men would most likely get right and five that women would? Is there a difference in the quality and/or status of the questions?

MEN
1.
2.
3.
4.
5.

WOMEN
1.
2.
3.
4.
5.

Student Activities

Activity 7d: 1950s TV

If you can, look at some extracts of British television from the 1950s. There are various archive web sites including screenonline from the bfi (www.screenonline.org.uk.) You can also find archive DVDs of old television programmes.

If you have watched or read about some of these earlier shows list the elements in the presenters that you have noted. These may include the class, the accent, dress code, language, as well as the way they are presented through technical factors such as lighting. These are important points because they tell us about the ideas they represent.

Activity 7e: Spot the Message

In order to investigate representation issues further take one or two of the case study quiz shows in the section on textual analysis (Section 6) or others you may have studied and see how an analysis of them can reveal the underlying messages and beliefs about society.

'I've started so I'll finish'

Conclusion

Popular cultural programmes like quiz shows appear to be rather low key and unimportant in the range of material that we see on television everyday. However, as you are now aware they can become the centre of fierce criticism and debate. Your study of this topic should have opened up the way that genres which are often derided in the press are actually part of the barometer of the type of society in which we live. Who is in control and who has power in deciding what is popular culture or what is meant by education are important and fundamental questions to ask. The answer may well differ depending upon whether you take a socio-economic approach or a socio-liberal approach to understanding the media (see Section 1).

Educational radicals, such as Paulo Freire in Brazil, have asked these questions in formulating their ideas about who defines education and sets the goal-posts. (Freire, 1972). We may take it for granted that education means recalling facts, but is this what makes an educated person? Aren't there other factors as well? However, if the mass media show us quiz contestants winning through mental recall of a particular range of knowledge are they supporting the belief that this is what is meant by education?

These are fundamental questions about our society.

Less seriously, in spite of all these concerns quiz shows are great fun and with their interactive nature, the pleasure we have of seeing a competitive match, our delight in answering the questions and seeing a winner, they will probably survive in one form or another as long as broadcasting survives.

You may not be a quiz show fan but you with the audience at home will be calling out the answers as you watch. This is the power and the pleasure of the interactive nature of quizzes.

Good Luck!

References

Freire, P. (1972) *Pedagogy of the Oppressed*, Harmondsworth: Penguin.

Conclusions and Additional Activities

8.1 Controlled Test

A Channel 4 Commission

A Commissioning Editor for Channel 4 has provided a brief for a company to come up with a new quiz show.

A.N. Other
Commissioning Editor
Light Entertainment
Channel 4
London
XXYY2244

From: Channel 4 Commissioning Editor Light Entertainment

To: Television Production Companies on the commissioning list

Dear All,

As you know we have had some difficulties with changing the presenter of *Countdown* after the death of Richard Whitely. We now need to consider replacing the show which is 25-years-old with something new.

We want to appeal to a teenage audience without dumbing down the quiz format. However, we want a more interactive format, perhaps using technology that appeals to teenagers.

Your proposal will cover areas, such as title, format, presenter, set design, target audience, length of programme, prizes, style of show, type of contestants and how selected, and how you would integrate new technology into the show.

Brief:

- Mid evening slot after Channel 4 news. (Please note competition schedules.)

- A celebrity presenter.

- Prizes should be of high value but not too large so as not to attract criticism from the press and regulator Ofcom.

- Target audience young 'adults'. (These are young with a good education, maybe students who might watch the news or be waiting to watch *Big Brother* and will be 'inherited' or pre-echoed into this programme.)

- Interactive technology.

Please deliver your proposal by...................................

A. N. Other

Channel 4 Commissioning Editor for Light Entertainment

8.1 Controlled Test (continued)

Tasks

1. Reply to the letter saying that you are interested and have a format ready.

2. Draw up the format in a report form (sub-headings and bullet points). Use the editor's letter and brief as your guide. Remember issues such as interactivity and representation. Make sure you address these in your proposal.

You will need to research the genre carefully as well as the audience.

3. Title Sequence

- Write a rationale for the opening title sequence covering areas, such as why you have chosen this title, the reasons for the colours, sound track, layout, lighting, how the presenter would be dressed, and so on.

  ↘ Draw a storyboard (maximum 10 frames) showing the opening title sequence.

  ↘ Give technical codes both visual and sound.

  ↘ Say how long each shot would last in seconds.

- In addition draw a plan of the studio layout to show the position of the contestants; presenter; and any other fixed part of the set. This would be like a bird's eye view.

4. Suggest a sponsor to help fund the show and say why this sponsor would be interested – what are the advantages for the sponsor? (N.B. Channel 4.)

5. The pilot show has been broadcast. **Write a review in a teenage magazine** (the choice is yours) which addresses points raised by the pilot. Evaluate its success in targeting its audience. Has it achieved its aim? Would there be any improvements possible? Take an angle on whether you approve or disapprove of quizzes.

6. Create a web page for the new quiz. Look at other web sites for quizzes for your research. It could have details of past contestant and prizes; a biography of your presenter; pictures; perhaps an interactive quiz; a blog spot, etc.

Extension Activity

Group Work

Make a pilot extract of the show. Maybe you could do this as part of a charity day to raise money.

More Activities

The following are more extended activities than those given at the end of each section. They could be used to practise the skills required for the controlled test. They are outlines and can be easily adapted to suit different abilities.

Student Activities

Activity 8a: BBC Quiz Pitch

You are a member of a small production company that has got an idea for a new quiz show. (The BBC has to use at least 25% of outside independent producers.)

You therefore pitch your ideas to BBC1. (Remember the BBC is a PSB – Public Service Broadcaster – and would not give large prizes.)

The pitch should include:

- The title.
- The format – how the quiz works.
- Ideas of presenter – who might it be? Why do you think they would be good?
- Types of contestant – are they celebrities or ordinary people? Young or old?
- The type of knowledge to be tested – such as general knowledge or a specific area such as sport.
- The sorts of prizes offered – money, glory, a car.
- The target audience – older people, teenagers?
- Scheduling – where you see it fitting in best in the time slots for BBC1

You may also include a set design. This would show the layout of the set, the logo and so on.

Extension Activity

If possible you could make a short extract of a sample programme to show how it would work. For this you would require technical help and perhaps the help of other departments such as drama/theatre studies.

Activity 8b: Discussion and Note Preparation

Choose one of the following titles on which to either prepare a presentation or contribute to a class discussion:

'Quiz shows provide good entertainment and education at the same time.' Discuss.

'Quiz shows provide opportunities for ordinary people to star and have their 15 minutes of fame. They are not elitist.' What do you think?

'Quiz shows should be abolished; they are open to all types of fraudulent activity and they play on the basic instinct of greed.' Do you agree?

'Quiz shows are cheap and easy to produce. They are just fillers in between better programmes?' Discuss.

'Quiz shows like game shows and reality TV reveal how much popular culture caters for the lowest common denominator and dumbs down society.' Discuss.

'Quiz shows are fun and allow audiences to interact with television.' Discuss.

Remember to use examples from your work on quiz shows and your reading to illustrate points you are making. You could find out more about particular quiz shows by doing research on the internet (see web sites in references).

Extension Activities

Write up your discussion in the form of an essay. Give both sides of the arguments.

Student Activities

Activity 8c: The Local Bugle

A new quiz show has just appeared in which a local resident is involved. Write an article for your local paper on: 'Television quiz shows'.

Before you start look at your local paper and research the style and type of language used and the average length of a feature article. Try to link your article to a current debate/programme to make it 'newsworthy' such as a local winner or a scandal. (These can be fictitious!)

A good article should have an angle – a point of view.

A good article will try to personalise the story (have someone on whom to hang the story) and link it to a local issue.

Remember this is not a news item but a feature article.

An article should include answers to: Who, What, Where and When in its opening paragraph.

Here are some ideas of what you might include:

- A bit of history/background.
- Examples of quiz shows.
- Controversy over phone-ins.
- Ideas about the role the quiz show plays today in television.
- What the audience gains from watching the show.
- A point about how drama and tension are part of the fun.
- What the contestants gain from participating – put in some quotes.

In conclusion: Do they benefit society or are they dumbing down society? Is there a 'moral panic' about quizzes? Are quizzes educational? What is your angle?

Extension Activity

Lay out the article in the form of a newspaper page with a headline and columns. There are software packages to help with layout. If you are making up a local winner you could insert a photo of yourself or a friend into the story or you could get an image from a search engine such as Google to illustrate the article.

Think of a good headline. Use sub-headings or cross-headings. Look for other layout devices, such as drop capitals, to make it visually interesting. Do not forget to put your by-line on the article.

Activity 8d: Your Specialist Subject Is?

Develop a quiz show format based upon a topic you are studying in a different subject such as history, geography or science.

Consider all the conventions suggested in the section on genre such as catch phrase, the set, sound, and so on.

You will need to think about the difficulty of questions, can you phrase them for quick answers like *Mastermind* or are you going to give multiple choice answers to choose from.

Consider a picture or sound round.

What format? Individual or team, like *The Weakest Link* with eight competitors starting off? Or maybe in a noughts and crosses format so the winning team is the first with a complete line of successful answers, etc.

Extension Activity

You could try the quiz out on your class in that subject. Ask the subject teacher to help.

You might like to consider a suitable prize if you have a winner(s).

Student Activities

Activity 8e: Title Sequence

Create a title sequence for a new quiz show targeted at children aged 11–14.

Consider using all or some of the following:

- Title – the name and the graphics involved.

- Logo – design a logo.

- Colours and lighting – are they going to be warm, bright, cool, dark?

- Images – what will you see in the frame?

- Style – will it be cartoonish, fast, clever, straightforward, colourful?

- Pre-recorded scenes – to give a taste of what is to come.

- Set and layout – will you see the set? What position will the camera be in?

- Music – what style? Will it be a song? Are the words appropriate?

- Voice over – would you have one? Would it be male or female? Old or young?

Extension Activities

Having made all these decisions, you can draw a storyboard; or digitally photograph the title sequence.

Image   shot no: [   ]   dialogue / sfx / music

_____

_____

_____

_____

shot duration (secs); _____

[   ]

_____

_____

_____

_____

_____

[   ]

_____

_____

_____

_____

_____

[   ]

_____

_____

_____

_____

_____

[   ]

_____

_____

_____

_____

_____

Student Activities

Activity 8f: Local Cable TV

A Commissioning Agent from your local cable station wishes to encourage student viewing around tea time. They believe a quiz show would be good.

They have asked you for a proposal for a new show:

- Consider what type of show would appeal to your community.
- Decide on title.
- Format.
- Technical codes such as lighting and colours.
- Types of contestant – celebrities, for example, might be too expensive.
- Presenter – who would appeal to this target audience?
- Setting/studio space – is this low or high budget?
- Audience participation or not – will they be able to help contestants? How?
- Prizes – what type and value?

Send the proposal in a form of a report to:

The Commissioning Producer
Local Cable TV
AnyPlace
Anytown
XX22 3YY

Extension Activity

Get your group to try out your idea. If there are several ideas vote for the one to which you would give the commission.

Activity 8g: A Make-Over

(N.B. Choose another quiz if more suitable.)

A Question of Sport is a long running celebrity quiz show. The producers believe the profile of its audience needs to be made younger. How would you achieve this? You will need to look at one broadcast of the programme and note down its present formula before attempting a make-over.

How would you give it a make-over?

Consider the following:

- Contestants.
- Presenter.
- Lighting.
- Set.
- Graphics.

Write a report on how these changed elements would help to attract a new younger audience.

Heading: 'A Report on *A Question of Sport* and Targeting a Younger Audience'

Sub-headings: Present Formula; What to Keep; What to Cut; Recommendations.

Remember a report can use bullet points rather than paragraphs. It can also use sub-headings.

Extension Activity

Print out your report for assessment by others in your media group.

Vote for the best proposal. (N.B. This doesn't mean the best writing – it's the best *idea*.)

Scheme of Work

This scheme of work provides a way of approaching teaching TV quiz shows as a contained module. The order of the material covered can be altered. For example, textual analysis (Section 5) depending upon background media knowledge might be more appropriate positioned earlier for some classes.

'Lesson' therefore refers to areas of study rather than specific timeslots.

Each 'lesson' could be completed over a week's lesson time depending upon number of hours allocated. Together they could cover a term's work.

The Activities are laid out at the end of each relevant section.

Each week an extract or the whole of one quiz show could be watched and analysed as part of the study period. Notes could be made using the activity work sheets in the textual analysis and genre sections to provide a bank of ideas and information. As quiz shows come and go no specific shows are referenced. Current shows will need to be recorded and used appropriately.

Lesson 1

Aim: To stimulate interest and provide resources.
Introduction: Section 1 Activities.
Brainstorm: What quiz shows do students watch?
Audience research on quiz viewers: Who watches what.
View one quiz show.
Homework: Collect listings for scheduling research.

Lesson 2

Aim: To give background to the development of quiz shows.
The History of Quiz Shows: Section 2 Activities.
Resources: *Quiz Show dvd* available from sites such as www.moviemail.com. (N.B. Could also

be used with Sections 4 and 7 (see later lessons).
Web sites on history of television: See end of section.
View one TV quiz show.
Homework: Research what relatives remember about quiz shows and what they watched, or do internet research.

Lesson 3

Aim: To understand audiences are not homogenous; how they use media texts.
Audiences: Section 3 Activities.
Explain audience theories of active and passive audiences, media effects and uses and gratification theories .
Pleasures of the genre; why people watch.
View one TV quiz show.
Homework: Primary research on audiences. See Introduction and Section 3 for tasks.

Lesson 4

Aim: To provide some knowledge of the structure of UK television and how it affects quiz shows.
Industries and Institutions: Section 4 Activities.
Concepts to cover:

- PSB and Commercial broadcasting.

- Working practices – Institutions.

- Regulation – Ofcom, BBC, ISCTIS.

- View one TV quiz show.

Homework: Research web sites of regulators for any recent comments on quiz shows, particularly phone-ins (see relevant section for web sites).

Lesson 5

Aim: To understand the structure of texts and practise analysing using semiotics.
Genre/Textual Analysis Section 5 Activities.
Watch a selection of extracts of different types of shows and tabulate similarities and differences.
View one whole quiz show to understand its overall structure opening/middle/closure.
Homework: Choose one programme and see

NOTES:

how it fits the genre table. In what way(s) does it differentiate itself from other shows such as a game show?

Lessons 6 and 7

Aim: To use case studies to show how genre and textual analysis work on a text.
Case Studies; Section 6 activities
Concept – semiotic analysis
Technical codes of camera; editing; lighting; colour; sound and mise-en-scène
The formula; the presenter; the competitors
Re-cap on quiz shows already watched and the different sub-genres in quiz shows

Use activities to look at title sequences.
How do they fit the formula? Compare results.
Watch *Starter for Ten* if available and other quiz extracts.
Homework: analyse the opening sequence of a given quiz show.

Lesson 8

Aim: to bring together the issues touched upon in studying quizzes to show how they can reveal power and values.
Debates Section 7 activities (*Quiz Show* could be used here)
Representation of different groups introducing stereotyping such as of class, gender, age, race, disability, ethnicity.
High and Low culture and its importance in setting values and power in society.
Dumbing down debate with respect to television
View the film *Quiz Show*.
Homework: write an essay on the issues raised by the film – see section 8

Lesson 9

Aim: Practise for controlled test.
Practice Papers
See section 8 for ideas.
Homework: prepare one of the activities to complete in class under timed conditions to cover all key concepts.

Lesson 10 Summative Work

Aim: Revision.
Revision of key concepts on audience, producers, genre and narrative, textual analysis, ideologies, regulation.
Do practice activities and/or Controlled Test for mock exam.
Homework: Learn Glossary/spelling of key words.
Complete one extension activity from Section 8.

Glossary

Glossary

Articulate – there are two meanings associated with this. To express, speak out and secondly to join with (as in an articulated lorry).

Audience – defines the readers of media texts and may be measured in terms of numbers, gender, class, education, income. There are two basic approaches: that of passive and active audiences (see narrowcast).

Barthes, Roland – an important writer on the media who developed the idea of five codes which can be used to analyse narrative in detail; as well as many other theories, such as types of pleasure which he termed jouissance and plaisir.

Catchphrases – a phrase repeated regularly which becomes associated with a personality and a particular quiz show.

Chiaroscuro – light and dark juxtaposed together as with a spotlight. Used with lighting and colour. Often seen in expressionistic texts and film noir.

Commercial television – television paid for by advertising or sponsorship.

Connotation/denotation – denote is the object/element and connote is what it suggests, the meanings it conveys.

Convergence – the joining together of different strands; in this case of media such as television, computers, and other forms of communication into one unit or VDU.

Culture – high/low – culture is a way of life but it is often value laden. Pop culture has less status than high culture such as classical music.

Demographics – how groups of people are organised socially and geographically.

Denote/connote – see connotation.

Diegesis – the world of the text.

Discourse – the ways that society is presented to itself through different media which connect together to develop a belief or representation (Michel Foucault).

Effects – the Media Effects model suggests that the media influences audiences and they react (passively) to this.

Encoding/decoding – putting elements together in a code is encoding this can then be read by the audiences as they de-code the structure (Stuart Hall).

Genre – refers to types of story or types of programme and products. There are common elements which create codes and conventions. Codes are necessary conventions can change.

Hegemony – this is a concept which sees the power of the media being part of the way that society is controlled to retain an equilibrium in favour of the dominant groups (Antonio Gramsci).

Ideology – beliefs, meanings and messages which are delivered through the media. They are 'false beliefs' in that they are not natural but socially constructed.

Inscribed – the way that audiences are 'written into' the text by positioning through camera, lighting, narrative, etc.

Institution – the media organisations and their working practices, such as the producers of television quiz shows.

Interactive – the ability to have two-way communication and responses.

Intertextuality – connections and references made across texts which add to the meaning of the text providing cultural and symbolic layers.

Jouissance – the word used by Roland Barthes to express extreme pleasure – sometimes translated as 'bliss' (see Plaisir).

Lévi-Strauss, Claude – an anthropologist who studied how narratives were made up of binary oppositions such as winner/loser.

Mediation – the action of re-presenting material to an audience on which the text is based. So editing can make someone appear powerful, intelligent or stupid through mediated construction.

Mise-en-scène – the organisation of the scene inside the frame with objects, composition, lighting, camera position and so on.

Narrative – story structures. How the story is organised and how the reader is positioned to understand the meanings of the story. Texts other than fictional stories, such as the news also have narratives.

Narrowcast/niche/mass audiences – a mass audience is reached by a broad, spatter approach; narrowcasting looks for more targeted audiences whilst niche is a very small audience interested in a very specific area.

Peak/prime time – the most important time for schedulers in the early evening where people are coming home from work, having tea and settling down for the evening, usually around 5 p.m. to 10 p.m. (8 p.m. is the core of this period).

Plaisir – everyday pleasure as opposed to extreme pleasure or jouissance (Roland Barthes).

Pluralistic – the idea that there are many voices and many meanings (polysemic) associated with reading media texts so that it is not monolithic.

Political-economic view – this suggests that the media are controlled by owners/political interests and audiences are powerless (see Social-liberal).

Preferred reading – the meanings and readings of the text are constructed to give the audience a preferred way of understanding. This is subconscious. Some members of the audience may read in a negotiated or oppositional way but in the mass media the preferred reading is usually dominant and underpins the dominant ideologies.

Propp, Vladimir – established important ideas about narrative through his study of fairy and folk stories, particularly the idea of seven character roles and 32 stages through which narratives move.

PSB (public service broadcasting) – established with the BBC it stands for education, information and entertainment. It is paid for by the public through a licence fee/tax/subscription and administered by a body independent of government.

Realism – the texts we consume in the media are not real. They are selected and constructed through choices made by producers. For example, the apparent reality of the news or a documentary is an illusion.

Representation – how groups are re-presented to us through the media and through repetition of ideas and simplification of issues (see stereotype).

Schedules – the way the day is divided up by broadcasters into slots for different audiences. The broadcasters use different devices in scheduling such as hammocking to attract and keep audiences to their channels. Time shifting through for example digital replays is leading to a more complex situation.

Semiotics/semiology – the study or science of signs. A sign signifies something – the signified. So a red rose (the sign) can signify amongst other things romance or patriotism (the signified) depending upon context.

Social-liberal – this position sees audiences as more powerful than the political-economic view in that they can choose to buy into texts and can

read them in alternative ways.

Stereotype – generalised and over simplified construction of groups. Assumptions about individuals are made which are based upon this group type. Their repetition can lead to negative and prejudiced beliefs.

Text – any piece of communication is a text. So a star or celebrity can be analysed as a text. For example, Roland Barthes semiotically analysed a famous Hollywood star's face, that of Greta Garbo.

Technological determinism – this idea is first associated with the work of Raymond Williams. He discussed how far the technology determined the media texts and how we used it, rather than the users determining it. The classic example is the printing press causing the establishment of a 'correct' way of spelling and writing, whereas before this invention spelling was regional if not individual.

Todorov – showed how narratives can be analysed in the way that equilibriums are disrupted and reconstituted in a narrative. This shows their ideological or mythic meanings as the new equilibrium reveals messages.

Uses and gratification theory – audiences have complex needs and use the media to gratify them. Needs have social origins such as tension which the media help to explore by providing escapism, or isolation where the media can provide companionship.

Vicarious – experiences which are second hand such as we experience through the media.

Voyeurism – ways of looking at icons and having the power over the image to look at them whilst what is being looked at is powerless.

Watershed – in the UK there is an agreement among broadcasters (not Sky who use 8 p.m.) that after 9 p.m. adult material can be shown and children watching after this point do so with the carer's consent.

References

References

Each chapter is referenced separately. This is a brief summary of some of the more useful sources for this area of study.

Allen, (1987) 'Audiences', in O'Sullivan, T., Dutton, R., Raynor, P. (eds) (2003) *Studying the Media*, London, Hodder, Arnold.

Berkmann, M. (1999) *Brain Men: A Passion to Compete*, London: Little, Brown.

Casey, B. (2002) *TV Studies: The Key Concepts*, London: Routledge.

Clarke, M. (1987) *Teaching Popular Television*, Oxford: Heinemann. [City of publisher?]

Creeber, G. (2002) *The Television Genre Book*, London: bfi.

Fiske, J. (1987) *Television Culture* (Chapter 14 'Quizzical Pleasures'), London: Routledge/Methuen.

Hoerschelmann, O. (2006) *Rules of the Game: Quiz Shows in American Culture*. New York: State University of New York Press.

Holmes, S. (2005) *British Television and Film Culture in the 1950s: Coming to a TV Near You*, Bristol, Intellect Books.

Holmes, S. 'The Quiz/Show in British TV History' www.birth-of-tv.org/birth/ 23 December 2005.

Holmes, S. (2005) '"It's a Woman?": The Question of Gender in *Who Wants to be a Millionaire*', *Screen Journal*, Vol. 46 (2), Summer.

Holmes, S. (2006)'The Question Is – Is it All Worth Knowing? The Cultural Circulation of the Early British Quiz Show', in *Media Culture and Society*, London: Sage Publications, vol. 29(1): 53–74.

Holmes. S. (2008) *The Quiz and Game Show*, Edinburgh: Edinburgh University Press.

Kruger, S. and Wall, I. (1992) *The Media Pack*, Basingstoke: Macmillan.

Masterman, L. (1985) *Teaching the Media*, London: Routledge.

McQuail, D. et al, (1972) 'The television audience: a revised perspective' in D. McQuail (ed.) *Sociology of Mass Communication*, London: Longman.

McQueen, D. (1998) *Television: A Media Student's Guide*, London: Arnold.

Mittell, J. (2004) *Television and Genre: From Cop Shows to Cartoons*, London: Routledge.

Media File Series 4 Issue 1 (1991) Mary Glasgow Publications Ltd.

Stone, J. and Yohn, T. (1992) *Prime Time Misdemeanors: Investigating the 1950s TV Quiz Scandal*, New Brunswick: Rutgers University Press.

Tedlow, R. (1976) 'Intellect on Television: The Quiz Show Scandals of the 1950s', *American Quarterly*, 28 (4): 483–95.

Wayne, M. (2000) 'Who Wants to be a Millionaire? Contextual Analysis and the Endgame of Public Service Television', in Fleming, D. (ed.) *Formations: A 21st Century Media Studies Textbook*, Manchester: Manchester University Press.

Web sites

www.ukgameshows.com – general site on quiz and game shows.

www.pbs.org – The American Experience/Quiz Show Scandal/People &Events/The Rise of TV Quiz Shows.

www.bbc.co.uk – a very useful site for general researching.

www.bbc.co.uk/weakestlink/ – the show's site.

www.barb.co.uk/viewing - summary of audience viewing figures.

www.ofcom.org.uk – the regulator of commercial broadcasting and communications.

www.guardianunlimited.co.uk – excellent newspaper site.

www.beonscreen.com – site for those wanting to take part in shows.

www.channel4.com/more4/quiz/index – refined site.

www.channel5.co.uk – channel site.

www.itv.co.uk – channel site.

www.whirligig-tv.co.uk – images of old TV shows.

Films

Starter For Ten (2006) Tom Vaughan, BBC Films.

Quiz Show (1994) Robert Redford, Hollywood Picture Company.